Mistakes, Misnomers and Misconceptions

R. BRASCH

Tynron Press
Scotland

First published by William Collins Pty Ltd
This edition published in 1990 by
Tynron Press
Stenhouse, Thornhill, Dumfriesshire DG3 4LD

© R. Brasch, 1983

ISBN 1-871948-53-3

Printed by Ludwinia Printer Pte Ltd, Singapore

For
ANDREW and TAMARA ADLER
in affection

"Friendship needs no words."
Dag Hammarskjold

Contents

and Fiddle — *The Pig and Whistle* — *The Swan with Two Necks* — A Parting Shot

3 *Optical Illusions —*
Things Are Not What They Appear 56

4 *Clerical Errors and Misprints* 61

5 *Sailing Under False Colours* 75

Camel's Hump — Glowing Eyes — Elephant Fallacies: Thick-skinned as an Elephant — White Elephant — Elephant Afraid of Mouse — Elephants Never Forget — Use of Trunk — Elephants' Burial Ground — Porcupines Shoot Their Quills — Squirrels and Their Store of Nuts — Vampires and Blood — The Mistaken Caterpillar — Centipedes — Bird Fallacies: Hen Laying Egg — To Eat Like a Bird — Free as a Bird — Bird-brained — Birds' Sleeping Habits — The Singing of the Nightingale — The Raven — As Blind as a Bat — Ostrich Burying Head in Sand — Ostriches Eat Anything — The Titmouse — Mass Suicide of Lemmings

10 Wrong Notions About the Famous 154

11 Obsolete Survivals 169

Foreword

Everyone knows that 'to err is human'. However, few people realize the profound role mistakes have played — for better or worse — in life. Many of them have become an integral part of civilization and everyday speech. It may be a consolation to know that even the most famous and learned — like a Shakespeare and an Aristotle — experts in their fields, were victims of error. They, too, blundered, misjudged situations and were misled. Unfortunately, because of their acknowledged authority, the mistakes they included in their works were accepted as indisputable truth. In many cases, they have never been rectified.

This book deals with the many facets of errors and the astounding variety of areas in which they have played a significant part. Not least, it tells the fascinating stories of how mere accidents came to enrich life. They led to the discovery of America and of penicillin and gave us frozen food, vulcanized rubber and dry-cleaning. It is an undeniable fact thus that mistakes, far from being harmful, proved beneficial. Almost paradoxically, it justifies the claim of the right to be wrong.

It is not surprising that former generations took seriously many a misconception. After all, they did not know better. But it makes one wonder how we, to this very day, take notions for granted that have long been outdated and proved fallacious.

Shingles are not caused by nerves and bagpipes are not Scottish. Neither does a cat's lick show affection nor do shifty eyes betray a person's untrustworthy character.

We really don't mean what we say when we speak of a bride 'walking down the aisle' or recall what happened when we were 'first married'. We never 'run' a temperature nor suffer from 'heartburn'.

So many of the terms we use are misnomers. They continue to misrepresent people, objects and concepts, as it were making them sail under false colours. There is nothing 'good' in Good Friday, and no one is ever drunk as 'blazes'. As the Danube is far from blue, so Greenland is mostly iced up. The turkey is an American bird, and Indian ink comes from China. Researching the phenomenon, we are led to strange and fascinating, but almost forgotten fragments of the past.

Misquotations have not only distorted what authors and sources said, but created erroneous attitudes and beliefs. Money was never condemned as the root of all evil nor was charity (as benevolent generosity) meant to start at home. Scots are not mean.

Misinterpretations constitute yet another category of mistakes (and a chapter of this book), showing how easily people can be misled with, at times, serious consequences.

There is much humour in errors as well, not merely in school howlers. When, in the early 1950s, migrants from Mytilene in the Mediterranean Sea, came to Australia, they formed their own association. They called it by the classical name of their Mediterranean home, 'The Lesbian Society of New South Wales'. It did not take long for the police to call on the (male) secretary to make inquiries. Did he admit, they asked, that they were Lesbians. Still limited in his mastery of English, the secretary did not realize the implication of the question and — long before modern 'gaiety' — confirmed the fact, 'Yes', he replied, they were Lesbians, 'and I am proud of it'!

The chapter on school howlers, Freudian slips and Spoonerisms portrays the great diversity in the causes and effects of errors. Just as they can reveal unexpected hidden motives, so they can prove a delightful source of hilarity. A mere accidental habit of the 'misplacement of words' can become an addiction, if not an obsession.

To mistake the identity of a person can be embarrassing, but a misinterpreted gesture or false accusation — whether innocently made or purposely contrived — like a doctor's wrong diagnosis, may result in anguish, if not in death.

All this, and much more, is contained in the book, leading the reader from simple optical illusions and clerical errors to astounding misconceptions and 'deadly mistakes'.

At some time or other we all make mistakes. It is unavoidable. Therefore, though it is good to be sure, it is most dangerous to be cocksure. 'My brethren,' said Oliver Cromwell, 'I beseech you ... think it possible you may be mistaken.' Whoever is convinced that he is always right, is not only a threat to himself, but a menace to others. No one is infallible.

To admit one's mistake shows wisdom and courage. Errors need not harm us. They are a test and a teacher. Some (like any lesson) cost money and others earn it (like misprints on postage stamps). However, as Confucius is alleged to have said, he who has committed an error and does not correct it, is making another mistake.

The study of mistakes goes far beyond a mere collection of misapplied or misunderstood words, terms and ideas. It is a study of man. What made him go wrong and why does he accept errors unquestioningly?

The pages that follow are meant to impart information on an extraordinary variety of subjects, all tied up with error. They are also intended to be read for pleasure by all those who enjoy the trivia of knowledge. They want to make the reader ponder and set his mind wandering on all kinds of unaccustomed trails and learn never to take things at their face value.

I cannot conclude this foreword without, once again, acknowledging the inestimable help my wife has given me in writing this book. My constant helpmate, enthusiastically and untiringly she has participated in every stage of its creation, pointing out many an error. However many errors I may have made in my life, of one thing I am certain: to have married her was an unmistakable blessing, the perfect choice of a mate who, with her manifold gifts, has staunchly stood by my side, sharing everything.

R.B.

1 It All Started By Accident or Mistake

History, science and medicine owe some of their milestones to so-called accidents. Without an error of judgment, a plan gone wrong, or an obvious fault or failure, discoveries might have been delayed by many centuries, diseases might still be unconquered and advances not taken place.

The many fruitful 'accidents' must make us wonder whether, after all, there might not be some pattern behind the apparently unplanned, unintended and unexpected. Mishaps may appear to us as such only because we do not understand them — yet. Anatole France once remarked, 'Chance is the pseudonym God uses when he does not want to sign his name.'

The phenomenon is so common that it is known by a special term, serendipity. The English author Horace Walpole coined the word in 1754. He took it from the Persian fairy tale, 'The Three Princes of Serendip'. (Serendip was the ancient name of Ceylon, the present-day Sri Lanka.) The heroes of the story possessed the gift of 'always making discoveries ... of things they were not in quest of'.

Bread

Our bread, prepared with sour dough or yeast, was unknown till about 2600 B.C. Like so many vital things, it was the result of an accident. Originally, bread was unleavened and therefore flat. An Egyptian slave entrusted with the task of baking bread, as usual, had

without yeast.

19

mixed water and flour into a dough which he had put into the oven. Perhaps it was a very hot day or he had worked too hard, but he fell asleep . . . On waking, to his consternation, he found that not only had the fire gone out, but the wafers had 'risen' to double their usual size.

Whilst he had been asleep, the warmth of the oven had fermented the mixture! Terrified of what his master would do to him, he tried to salvage the dough. He relit the fire, hoping that the heat would return the now large loaves to their former flat shape. Instead, they further increased in size and baked to a crusty golden brown.

Having no alternative, he served the 'spoiled' bread to his master who — against all expectation and fear — relished it! In fact, he praised the slave for his culinary art and ordered him henceforth to serve him the same type of bread daily.

Butter

It has been suggested that the first butter in the world was a chance-product man owes to the camel.

Camel riders covering vast distances, used to carry their milk supply with them. This they kept in leather containers which they loaded on the animals. The camels' rolling gait along the desert stretches churned the milk which had become sour, transforming it into butter.

Frozen Food

Meat shipped from Australia unexpectedly froze and on arrival was discovered to have kept so well that the 'accident' was adopted as a method, giving birth to modern refrigeration.

A patent for the new freezing process was taken out by the Australian engineer Eugene D. Nicolle in 1861. The first refrigerated cargo dispatched from Sydney to London reached its destination unspoiled and in a most satisfactory condition on the *Strathleven* in 1880. It was one of Australia's gifts to the world — bestowed quite by chance.

Saccharin

Saccharin which for many years has been of great benefit to those not permitted sugar, was not the result of scientists' search for a sugar substitute. It, too, came about by chance.

When one night in 1879, C. Fahlberg came home from his laboratory at Johns Hopkins University and, as usual, sat down for his evening meal, eating a slice of bread he could not make out its peculiar sweet taste. Scientifically trained, he took nothing for granted. In no time, he ascertained that there was no change in the bread. The sweetness therefore had to come from another source. Although he had washed his hands before leaving work, he realized that, from experiments he had made (together with his colleague Ira Remsen) on that day, some sweet-tasting substance must have stuck to his hands which somehow he had transferred to the bread.

Forgetting all about his food, he returned at once to the laboratory. He examined every test-tube, beaker and instrument they had used that day. His thrill knew no bounds when he was able not only to trace the substance, but to identify it as a by-product of coal tar. Its sweetness exceeded that of cane sugar almost 550 times! A practical man, he did not stop there. Aware of the product's dietetic value, he and Remsen lost no time in presenting saccharin to the world. They chose saccharin as its name from the ancient Sanskrit description of 'sugar'!

Cognac

'One cannot improve upon perfection' say the brandy makers. And cognac, this world-famous grape brandy — so Frenchmen claim — was the result of their country-men's contempt for the inferior, and of pure chance.

Peasants who lived near the river Charente, on which the town of Cognac is situated, had an overabundance of white wine. It was of such poor quality that to sell it locally was out of the question. They decided to send it to markets further away, less discriminating in taste.

However, as transport was costly, to do so would not have been worth the expense. Shrewdly they solved the problem. They reduced the large volume of the consignment by boiling down the wine. The result was most unexpected: the cheap wine had turned into the first cognac thus created by accident.

Granny Smith Apples

'Granny Smith' apples are another Australian gift to the world. They also came about by accident, in every sense of the word. There are several versions as to how they were first 'cultivated' in a now densely-populated Sydney suburb.

In the 1860s, the Smith family — migrants from England — had settled in Eastwood. To make a living, they grew vegetables and fruit. Maria Ann, Thomas Smith's wife, (affectionately known as 'Granny Smith') used to sell the produce on the Sydney markets.

One day (in 1868) she brought home some empty fruit cases of which one still contained a few rotting Tasmanian French Crab apples. She tipped them out on to the rubbish heap in the corner of their orchard. (One account locates the site near the creek that ran past their property.)

When some time later, 'Granny Smith' saw a small tree growing out of the 'dump', she transplanted it. In due course it bore fruit, apples that not only differed completely from any known so far, but surpassed them in taste.

According to another story, the first 'Granny Smith' apple tree grew and bore fruit quite unnoticed, till one day a small boy passing by, picked one of its apples. It was the best apple he had ever eaten. He shared his discovery with Granny Smith. An astute woman, she lost no time in transplanting and grafting the new, fortuitously created 'variety' of apple-tree and commercialized it.

There is yet a third tradition of how it all happened. This claims that a fruit agent had provided Granny Smith with samples of some green-coloured apples, known as the Tasmanian French Crab. He suggested to her that they might make good cooking apples. She took up his idea and, while preparing them for the cookingpot, carelessly threw their cores and peels out of the window, where they fell on to a flowerbed. Her thoughtless action led to the growth of the first tree to bear the apples.

The cases in which the apples were packed, were labelled 'Apples from Granny Smith'. Soon people everywhere asked for 'the Granny Smith', an apple and a name that grew into world fame. It is yet another fascinating example of what can happen by chance.

The Discovery of America

For millennia man imagined that the earth was a circular flat plate. Anyone who dared to sail beyond its rim would therefore fall off into an endless abyss. In Columbus' days this view had been disproved. The world was round! Columbus thus rightly reasoned that, even when sailing westward, by encircling the world he was bound to reach India in the East and do so long before those travelling the traditional land route. (It was not mere adventurous spirit that prompted him, but economic motives. Proving the feasibility of such voyage, he would greatly expedite the import of the highly-prized Indian spices!)

That is how, by accident, he discovered the New World! Nevertheless, we continue to speak of *Red Indians* and the *(West) Indies*. They are a living monument to the fruitfulness of mistakes.

The White House

The White House received its name only 'accidentally'! It was built in 1799 by James Hoban, an Irish architect who had migrated to America. In its design he copied the style of buildings he nostalgically remembered from back home, using grey sandstone. John Adams, the second President of the United States, was its first resident.

During the 'War of 1812' the British attacked the

building. Setting it on fire (on 24 August 1814), they almost totally destroyed it. All that was left were its bare, charred walls.

When hostilities ceased, Hoban was commissioned to restore the house. As it was impossible to remove the smoke stains from the grey sandstone, he decided to cover them up. He did so by painting the entire building white. Thus, as the result of mere repair work, the 'White House' came into being, though this description for the residence of the President of the United States was officially adopted only much later, by President Theodore Roosevelt.

The Spencer

Most people will throw away objects that are broken, torn or spoilt. Others, parsimoniously, will try to rescue whatever there is left. This practice is not confined to the impecunious.

Lord Spencer (1758-1834), certainly, belonged to the wealthy class of aristocratic Britain. A rather eccentric gentleman, he loved to be admired for his exquisite clothes and always to look spick and span.

On a cold English winter's day, so the story goes, he was warming his back in front of a roaring fire. At the time, he was wearing his latest suit, made of the finest of cloth and perfectly cut. He must have been too close to the fire, as the flames caught the tail of his coat which, before the fire could be put out, was badly damaged.

In spite of his wealth, Spencer was not prepared to sacrifice the entire coat. Summoning his tailor, he instructed him to trim off the charred and damaged parts and then neatly to finish off the remainder. The tailor duly accomplished the task. The result was a totally different sort of jacket. It was tailless, tightly fitting, and reached just below the waist.

It immediately caught people's attention who had never seen anything like it before. As it was then the custom to ape nobility in whatever they did or wore, it did not take long for the public to adopt the coat, displayed by so famous a person. Inevitably, it was called after its first wearer. 'The Spencer' became a popular garment with both sexes and, in some form or another, survives to this day.

Patterned Cloth

If a nobleman, who could well afford to dispense with a damaged frock coat, did not do so, it is all the more understandable for anyone not blessed with an abundance of money, to refuse to throw away a flawed product.

This applied to a weaver who, to his horror, noticed that fabric he had just woven showed imperfection. As the expensive material was of one colour, the fault was all the more conspicuous. For him to discard the cloth was out of the question. It would have meant too great a financial loss. Ingeniously thus, he set about to cover the 'fault' by adding a stripe of a different colour. This proved a welcome change for the patternless, plain cloth, which now looked so much more attractive. It caught on and by (correcting) a mistake, a new fashion was set, that of patterned cloth! It proves the veracity of the proverb that 'necessity is the mother of invention' and once again shows how productive even a fault can be.

Dry-cleaning

Many a beautiful dress has been ruined by an accident! But it was an accident as well that led to the discovery of its remedy — the process of dry-cleaning. Traditions vary as to the nature of the mishap.

According to one story, the unfortunate (but eventually lucky) victim was a tailor who fell into a vat of turpentine. When retrieved and having recovered from the shock, he looked at himself, and was most pleasantly surprised. His previously grubby clothes, miraculously had turned perfectly clean ...

A second account links the 'discovery' with a dinner

party, at which a guest had spilled some of his drink on the tablecloth. Embarrassed, he apologized to the hostess, who told him that there was no need for him to worry. In fact, she was greatly indebted to him. An observant lady, she had noticed that the spirit of the spilled drink had removed a stain on the cloth, no previous attempt on her part had succeeded in getting out. This set the stage for a new industry.

More definite in every detail is a third version. In 1849, during his wife's absence, Monsieur M. Jolly-Bellin, a Paris tailor, knocked over a spirit lamp. Fortunately it was not lit at the time. Nevertheless, he was greatly upset because, in the process it had spilled all its contents on his wife's favourite and freshly ironed tablecloth. Apprehensive of her return, he carefully examined the cloth, to find out what the accident had done to it. He could not believe his eyes when he saw that, instead of leaving a large dirty stain, the turpentine spirit having been soaked up by the cloth, made that very spot look so much cleaner. Greatly relieved, he did not leave it at that. An adventurous man, he started experimenting with the accidentally discovered properties of the spilled spirit to develop the first dry-cleaning establishment which became a most lucrative adjunct to his tailoring business.

Vulcanized Rubber

When the Scottish chemist Charles Macintosh had produced the world's first waterproof cloth, it was a boon to man. His novel 'macks' (which he patented in 1823) proved a welcome protection against the wet. However, a flaw soon became apparent, as it were a chink in the armour. Though the rubbery substance was resistant to rain, when exposed to extreme cold and changes of weather it became brittle and stiff.

The American inventor Charles Goodyear was determined to remedy the defect and find some way to render the rubber more pliable. For this purpose he embarked (in 1839) on a series of experiments. In their pursuit, he upset a bowl which contained a mixture he had prepared for the tests, accidentally spilling its contents on a hot stove. Clearing up the mess, Goodyear discovered that the heat had made the rubber elastic! Once again, an accident had turned out to be a blessing and to be responsible for a significant technological advance. In search of a name for the process, Goodyear called it vulcanization. The name (which he patented in 1844) recalled Vulcan, once worshipped by the Romans as their god of fire. The warmth of fire, indeed, had provided Goodyear with his invention.

Photography

It has always been man's desire to capture a fleeting moment, to keep it, if possible, not only for himself, but for generations to come.

The invention of the camera seemed to fulfil his wish. However, as soon as the 'photographs' (imprinted on glass plates coated with silver and sensitized by iodine vapour) were exposed to light, they vanished. He just could not 'fix' them — till one day (in 1837) an accident happened and a French painter — Louis Daguerre — stumbled on the secret of photography.

He used a camera obscura as an aid for his painting, but was greatly handicapped by the brief lifespan of the photographs. To hold their image permanently, he embarked on countless experiments, but one after the other proved a failure. To clear the desk, he deposited the exposed plates from his abortive tests into a chest, together with chemicals he intended to use later on to clean the plates for re-use.

When one day he opened the chest, he found to his surprise that one of the photographic plates showed a distinct picture, previously not visible. He was certain that one of the chemicals must have been responsible for it. Systematically he tested each in turn. But to no avail. Disappointed he was about to give up, when he noticed that some mercury had spilled into the chest. He immediately guessed that its vapour had 'developed' the photograph. His conjecture proved right and, in co-operation with Joseph Niepce, led to the invention of 'permanent' photography.

Dynamite

Dynamite was discovered not with a bang, but through a leak! Nitroglycerine, which had first been produced (in 1847) by the Italian Ascanio Sobrero, proved extremely dangerous to handle. When subjected to the slightest shock, it could wreak havoc. The Swedish chemist Alfred Nobel was determined to find a method to keep the devastating powers of the explosive under control. For this purpose he carried out numerous experiments.

The Swedish authorities did not welcome his work, as it had caused serious accidents and even death. His own brother had been killed when (in 1864) Nobel's workshop blew up! Not surprisingly, the government refused him permission to rebuild it on its former site. However, anxious to continue his tests, Nobel decided to do so away from populated areas, on a barge anchored at the centre of a lake. He did not realize then that he had set the stage for his — accidental — invention of dynamite.

On 14 July 1866, he became aware that one of the containers storing nitroglycerine had sprung a leak. Oddly however, the heavy oily liquid had been absorbed by the Kieselguhr box in which the containers were kept. (Kieselguhr was a sort of clay, formed from the remains of minute plants, which had already shown its value in chemistry by its absorbent porous qualities.)

Nobel noticed that in the process the Kieselguhr had stayed dry. The implication of the phenomenon did not escape him. What elaborate experimentation had failed to find, an accident, as it were, had thrown into his lap! By pure chance — a leakage — he had found the very substance that would make the volatile explosive safe. Without losing or diminishing any of its explosive power, combined with Kieselguhr, nitroglycerine could be harnessed. Thus kept in check, only the application of a detonator could set it off.

All that was left to do was to give 'Nobel's Safety Powder' a telling name. Nobel coined it himself (in 1867). He called it 'dynamite' — from the Greek *dunamis* — to highlight the enormous innate 'force' of the substance.

A widespread popular misconception linked with the discovery asserts that Nobel established (what was to become known as) the 'Nobel Prize for Peace' as an act of atonement for the horrendous suffering his invention was to bring when used in warfare. Nothing could be further from the truth. To start with, his invention proved of great benefit in various fields of human endeavour, particularly so in mining and construction. It was not penitence that prompted him to make the endowment, but his genuine and intense hatred of war.

Stainless Steel

Stainless steel was born on the scrap-heap! During the First World War, corrosion occurring in rifle barrels presented a serious problem. The government commissioned metallurgists to search for an alloy that would resist this costly deterioration which potentially could delay, if not endanger, the Allies' victory in battle.

All their experiments, however, seemed to prove futile, and thus barrel after barrel was thrown away. When one of the scientists passed the by then considerable scrap-heap, he noticed that some of the discarded tubes had not rusted. He immediately realized the importance of the 'find'. The accidental observation led to the invention of stainless steel.

Scotch Tape

A mishap in the production of a new, fashionable bi-coloured (1926) model of car resulted in (the naming of) Scotch tape. To ensure a neat line where the two colours met, the painters used a masking tape. Supplied by the Minnesota Mining and Manufacturing Company (the

3M), it served the purpose perfectly. Without effort, its adhesive side (5cm in width) could be stuck to the surface. However, 3M soon realized that to produce the tape was too costly. To make it a paying proposition, they decided to coat not the entire tape with glue, but merely its edges. The idea proved unsuccessful as, insufficiently glued, the tape fell off and the envisaged neat edge became smudged all over. Annoyed about the mess the tape had caused to their work, the painters asked the representatives of 3M to take 'this *Scotch* tape back to those bosses of yours and tell them to put adhesive all over it, not just on the edges'. Their angry description (using the so unjustified myth of the Scotsmen's meanness) has stuck to the tape ever since.

The Conquest of Beriberi

For centuries beriberi was a sickness that haunted people, particularly in Asian countries where rice was the staple food. Medical research just could not trace the organism suspected to cause the debilitating disease. An accidental occurrence (in 1896) then led to the cure, finding it in an entirely unexpected direction.

Dr Christiaan Eijkman, a Dutch physician who was engaged in pathological research at the Medical School of Batavia (the present-day Djakarta), used chickens for his experiments. All of a sudden these showed the very symptoms of the evasive disease. Attempts on his part to discover the cause and identify the mysterious germ proved abortive. And then, as quickly and unexpectedly as the disease had started, it disappeared.

The conscientious and scientifically trained doctor, however, was determined not to give up his quest. His zeal paid off. He discovered a strange coincidence of dates. It was linked with the hiring of a new hospital cook. Very economically-minded, he had discontinued his predecessor's practice to feed the chicken 'guinea-pigs' with unpolished rice, specifically purchased for the patients. Scraps, he felt, were good enough for the fowl.

The outbreak of beriberi occurred soon after the change of diet.

Experimentation confirmed his suspicion. Thus, by mere chance as it were, beriberi was conquered, and the entirely new concept of dietary deficiencies added to medical knowledge.

Penicillin

Penicillin was discovered by Sir Alexander Fleming through what could be termed an accident. Working at the bacteriological laboratory of St Mary's Hospital, London, he was studying a problem far removed from anything connected with the future drug. A culture of staphylococcus germs he was growing in his investigation somehow became contaminated. He could have easily thrown away the dish. Instead, he was intrigued by the green mould and its effect on the surrounding germs. Further examining the phenomenon, Fleming laid the ground of what was to become one of the twentieth-century wonder drugs.

Recalling the historic occasion of receiving his knighthood in 1944, Sir Alexander remarked, 'Like many other bacteriologists, I have had many culture plates contaminated with mould spores which drop in from the air, and like every other bacteriologist, I have cast them out with suitable expressions of annoyance; but on this one occasion I did not cast it out, and penicillin was the result. It seems to me, as it must seem to you, most extraordinary that a stray mould spore, coming from no one knows where, settling in St Mary's Hospital, should eventually have led to such phenomenal results.'

Anticoagulants

Thousands of people who have suffered a coronary occlusion which once would have proved fatal, now survive and can lead normal lives. They do so because of a mere accident.

In the state of Wisconsin, USA, cattle had

mysteriously died. Investigation traced their death to contaminated hay, on which they had fed. Further research (by Dr Karl P. Link of the University of Wisconsin in 1941) was able to identify 'dicumarin' as the substance that had brought about their death. Unaccountably, it had thinned the animals' blood — with fatal effect. There is no ill wind that does not blow someone some good. The discovery led to the development of anticoagulants which proved such extraordinary life-savers. Thus man owes yet another of the modern 'miracle drugs' to the phenomenon of serendipity!

LSD

Modern man embarked on his first psychedelic trip quite by chance! A mere fluke created LSD.

In 1943, a young Swiss scientist, Albert Hofmann, was investigating the effects of ergot on haemorrhage and the nervous system. During the experiments some of the substance got stuck to his fingers with which unintentionally he touched his lips. In no time, he experienced hallucinations and a sense of euphoria, which lasted for the rest of the day.

A trained scientist, he immediately set to work to find out the reason for the phenomenon which had come his way so unexpectedly and accidentally. It resulted in his discovery of the hallucinogenic potency of the drug.

Its common description (by initials) as LSD is rather an odd mixture and in itself confusing. Meant to represent *l*ysergic *a*cid *d*iethylamide, the central 's' makes no sense. How did it take the place of the 'a' in *a*cid? There is a simple explanation. It was not due to a mistake, but to an apparently strange choice on Hofmann's part. He spoke German and the German for acid is *sauer*. For some reason, best-known to him, he chose its initial in preference to that of the acid and thereby created the hybrid of LSD.

Cortisone

Not a few benefits to mankind were the by-products of major wars. One such boon is the synthetic hormone cortisone, used so effectively in the treatment of rheumatoid arthritis and skin diseases. Its production was due to an unfounded rumour!

During the Second World War intelligence reports reached the United States claiming that to enable German pilots to fly for extended periods at altitudes of 40,000 feet (approximately 13,000 metres) they were given a special substance extracted from the adrenal gland of cattle.

Though it turned out that the information was incorrect, it was the incentive to make Dr Edward C. Kendall, a biochemist at the famous Mayo Clinic, speed up his research. For some time he had suspected hormones to possess healing qualities, particularly a substance known as Compound E. So far, this could be obtained only in minute quantities. If it could be produced in large amounts, it would be of tremendous therapeutic value.

Urged on by the government and assisted by several colleagues, he continued his research, culminating in 1946 in the synthesizing of the hormone which they named cortisone. Kendall compared its discovery with the finding of a pearl of great beauty in the murky depth of the sea.

The Hallelujah Chorus

An accidental incident was responsible for a tradition now observed at every performance of Handel's *Messiah*. The entire audience stands up for the Hallelujah chorus.

It is generally believed that the custom can be traced to the impact of Handel's oratorio, when first heard in London in 1743. Those present were so deeply affected by the glorious passage that, spontaneously, they had risen from their seats and had remained standing to the end of the chorus.

The story is apocryphal. The actual reason is said to be very mundane and it has several versions.

On one occasion, King George II and his family had been late for the performance, entering the royal box at the very moment the *Hallelujah* was about to be sung. Their arrival did not go unnoticed and, in deference to the royal visitors, all present immediately rose to their feet. They remained standing till the king and his party were seated. By mere chance, this coincided with the conclusion of the chorus.

Another explanation, very much less reverently, asserts that it all started with 'a king' (often identified with George I) falling asleep during a performance of Handel's work. Possibly roused by the chorus, he woke up. He was so startled that, without even realizing what he was doing, he rose to his feet. Naturally, everyone present though not knowing why, followed the royal example.

Somehow, the reason (whichever it was) was forgotten and, ever since, audiences consider it proper to rise when the *Hallelujah* is sung.

The American Baseball 'Stretch'

More recent and yet of similar nature is the American custom at their national game of baseball to take a 'stretch' after the seventh inning. The usual — but erroneous — explanation bases the practice on very practical considerations. Having sat for some time on not always too comfortable benches, spectators need to get up and 'stretch'.

It all started, however, in totally different circumstances, this time not in deference to a king but, in republican America, to honour a president. Herbert Hoover who was attending a game, for reasons unknown or forgotten, had to leave before it was finished. It so happened that his departure coincided with the end of the seventh inning. Seeing their president leave, all spectators got up to pay him respect. This is the origin of the 'stretch' which has been observed at that very juncture of every game ever since.

'Silent Night, Holy Night'

'Silent Night, Holy Night', the favourite Christmas hymn, originated by accident! It was created for an emergency, on the spur of the moment, and owes its very existence to the proverbial, but in this case very real, church mice!

On Christmas eve of 1818, Father Josef Mohr, the priest of the Austrian village of Oberndorf, was preparing his church for the solemn midnight Mass. To his consternation he discovered that the organ was out of order. Looking for the cause, he found that part of its leather bellows had been eaten away by mice. Time was too short to have the damage repaired.

Father Mohr felt that without organ music the service would lose much of its beauty and warmth. Something had to take its place. He had written a Christmas poem which he now rushed to Franz Gruber, the local schoolmaster, who was also the church organist, an amateur composer and, like himself, played the guitar. Mohr asked him whether he could quickly set his poem to music, so that it would be ready that very night. He should do so for two solo voices to be accompanied by guitars. Gruber gladly obliged. It took him a few hours to compose the tune of the hymn which was to conquer the world. 'Silent Night, Holy Night' was thus sung for the first time on the very night of its rapid composition — by the two men in that little village church.

Soon the hymn captivated the hearts and minds of many Christians far beyond Oberndorf. The renowned Zillertal choir made it part of the recitals it gave all over the country, popularizing the hymn nationwide. Almost 100 years later, Bing Crosby gave it world fame.

2 Misheard

A common cause of an error is very simple. People misunderstand what has been said. Something once misheard may never be corrected and give rise to false concepts and erroneous traditions, many of which have become permanent features of our culture.

Much of knowledge consists of mere hearsay, and everyone is aware of its unreliability. Surprising therefore is the number of misunderstandings which now are an integral part of the vocabulary, the phraseology and attitudes of everyday life.

Misheard names, statements and affirmations have obscured, if not distorted, meanings. They have also provided a large area of entertaining and, at times, amusing research. This extends far beyond such minor mistakes as calling the Babylonian king Nebuchadrezzar — Nebuchadnezzar and misrepresenting Moctezuma, the Aztec king, as Montezuma. Though the mispronunciation of their names is of very little significance today, it would have had major consequences in their life-time.

'Birds and Bees'

To speak of 'birds and bees' once was a euphemism for discussing the sex act. If used at all nowadays, it is done in a light-hearted, jocular way. But the very phrase presents a problem. Why, of all creatures, should birds and bees be singled out to describe the process of procreation?

Some authorities have suggested that it goes back to the days, when sex instruction was a taboo subject. To teach children 'the facts of life', nature study took its place. Children were told how birds hatched eggs and bees pollinated flowers. The rest was (hopefully) left to the children's imagination.

It is a rather unconvincing explanation. After all, there were so many better examples near at hand. Children, always observant, were well aware of the sex play and copulation of pets and other domestic animals, which could have served as a much more suitable 'lesson'. There was no reason therefore to seek out 'the birds and the bees'.

The strange combination might well be the result of a misheard word from a once popular hymn for evensong. This had been written by Sabine Baring-Gould, clergyman-author of the well-known hymn 'Onward Christian Soldiers', and was particularly loved by children. It portrayed the arrival of night:

> Now the day is over,
>   Night is drawing nigh,
> Shadows of the evening
>   Steal across the sky ...
> *Birds and beasts* and flowers
>   Soon will be asleep.

Somehow — perhaps through slovenly enunciation — the beasts came to sound like bees, and thus misheard (and contracted) contributed to the creation of the proverbial 'birds and bees'.

That the phrase may be traced to the Rev. Baring-Gould is especially fascinating, if it is realized that he was not only the prolific author of 159 books, but also father of fourteen children.

Good Friday

Almost paradoxically, the anniversary commemorating Christ's crucifixion is known as 'Good Friday'. How could so gloomy a day in the Christian calendar ever be called 'good'?

It has been suggested that 'good' referred to the

consequences of the crucifixion. According to Christian dogma, Jesus' death on the cross brought atonement for man's original sin. Hence, *good,* after all, had come out of evil. Others have seen in the 'good' a mere alternate for 'holy'. However, most likely, Good Friday is a corruption of 'God's Friday' — a name misheard.

The White Rhinoceros

Even when not wallowing in mud, a 'white' rhinoceros is not white. In fact, its brownish-grey colour is no paler than that of its more common 'black' relative. Its name, indeed, is based on a misunderstanding.

The two species differ in their feeding habits. The black rhinoceros seeks its food in thorny bushes, for which purpose nature provided it with a pointed upper lip. The so-called white rhinoceros, on the other hand, lives on siliceous grasses. To facilitate grazing, its nose is flat while its lips are square and wide. This made the South African Boer refer to the animal as the *wide-*(nosed) one. Englishmen, not familiar with the Afrikaans language, mistook the *wijd* (for 'wide') to mean 'white' and that is how, by mishearing, the white rhinoceros came into being.

The Elephant's Trunk

The elephant's trunk has no (linguistic) connection with the trunk once used to pack personal effects when going on a trip. Like the American trunk of a car, its root goes back to a tree-trunk which, hollowed out, served as the early suitcase or strongbox.

The elephant's trunk comes from the Old English *trump,* for 'trumpet'! This follows the ancient Romans' description of the animal's elongated nasal part. They had called it after the musical instrument because — as Livy, the famous Roman author, explained — 'The elephant can make a noise like a trumpet'. The English eventually garbled the sound of the trump(et) to produce the elephant's trunk.

Raining Cats and Dogs

Several explanations have been given for the description of a heavy downpour as 'raining cats and dogs'. They range from the misheard Greek word for a waterfall (*catadupa*) to faulty reasoning. After a cloudburst and flash-flooding, drowned cats and dogs used to float down London streets. The simple-minded imagined these to have come down with the rain from the skies.

Most probably, however, the phrase goes back to German migrants to America who had settled in south-eastern Pennsylvania. Their English was hard to understand.

Heavy showers reminded them of a popular saying 'back home'. It spoke of raining so much that it kept in the cats and brought out the ducks. In their strong German accent the ducks sounded very much like dogs. Those listening to them, puzzled by what they were talking about, misunderstood them to say that it was raining cats and dogs. The strange combination of two pets that usually keep strictly apart, made the bizarre phrase all the more memorable.

The Stormy Petrel:
Mother Carey's Chickens

When sailors on the high seas first observed a small bird skimming the waves with its long, pointed wings, they imagined that it was dipping its feet into the water. It seemed to them as if the bird was running along the surface of the sea. This reminded them of the Gospel story (Matth. 14,29-31), in which St Peter left his boat on the Sea of Galilee to walk on its waters towards Jesus. So they called the bird after the apostle. But because it was so small a creature, they used for it the more affectionate, diminutive of his name 'little Peter', Peterel. In Italian this was Petrello, a name which eventually contracted into the petrel!

The sailors also noticed that the bird attached itself to the boat particularly during rough weather, when a

hurricane blew. This made them speak of it as 'the stormy
petrel', a description adopted worldwide.

The seamen were puzzled. What accounted for the
bird's sudden presence? The most obvious explanation
that it sought shelter in the lee of the ship, did not satisfy
their superstitious minds. They believed it was a messen-
ger. Soon confusing the sequence of events, they assumed
that the stormy petrel had been sent by the Virgin Mary
to give them warning of impending danger.

At the time, Catholics still used Latin and Mary, 'the
beloved mother', was known to them as *Mater Cara*.
Fondly they therefore referred to 'her' birds as 'Mater
Cara's chickens'. When the Latin words became
incomprehensible to the sailors, they mistook them to
mean 'Mother Carey's chickens'. Eventually the new
name — the result of faulty hearing — was applied to
anyone whose arrival seemed to coincide with imminent
trouble.

In another version, the birds were seen as the envoys of
a powerful sea-witch, doing her bidding. Destructive
storms were ascribed to her. She created them to bring
havoc to ship and crew. Sailors were so scared of her that
they did not dare to utter her name as in doing so, they
thought, they would conjure her up and prompt her all
the more to do her nefarious work. Hence, whenever they
spoke of the witch, they referred to her by the name of the
Virgin Mary, Mater Cara who, surely, would not mind
her name to be used to protect her faithful children. If,
however, the witch were to discover their ruse, the sailors
further reasoned, she would feel flattered and refrain
from harming them. Inevitably the deceptive name was
equally used for what were considered the witch's birds.

The Foxglove

Intriguing, indeed, is the name of the foxglove. Its shape
does not show the slightest resemblance to a fox, nor do
foxes feed on the flower. Its description is a typical case of
confusion of sound.

Botanically known as *digitalis purpurea,* the plant has helped millions of people suffering from heart disease. Appropriately, the drug obtained from it is called after the flower — *digitalis.*

Early on, it was believed that the plant had received its mysterious pharmaceutical power from supernatural beings, the 'little folks'. It was their flower and because of their proprietary rights, it was called the (little) 'folks' glove. Obviously the 'glove' part of the name was suggested by the shape of the flower's bell-like blossoms.

Misheard, the folks-glove changed into the foxglove. This was in keeping with a society which had lost faith in the existence of those little folk of the occult world.

The Fleur-De-Lis

The fleur-de-lis, famous emblem of France and, until 1801, also part of the royal arms of England, has been the victim of much confusion. Not surprisingly, authorities have questioned its very meaning. Though obviously speaking of a flower (the French *fleur*), even this has been doubted by some who claimed that the symbol was not floral at all, but represented the top of a sceptre, lance or battle-axe. However, it is now assumed that it depicted a species of iris, botanically classified as *iris florentina.*

The *lis* part in its name created a further problem. It seemed to make no sense. And rightly so as, in fact, it is the result of an early misunderstanding.

Soon after setting forth on his Crusade to the Holy Land in 1146, King Louis VII of France adopted the iris as the royal ensign. Thus it became known as 'the flower of (King) Louis', *fleur de Louis.* With the passing of time (and the king), the royal association of the emblem was forgotten and, no doubt, slovenly speech caused the 'de Louis' to sound like 'de lis'. The *fleur de Louis* had become the 'fleur de lis'! The new description mystified and misled people. (No wonder that even Shakespeare used a corrupted version current at the time, speaking of the 'flower-de-luce'.)

This was not the end of misunderstandings. The iris was now imagined to be a lily, a fallacy suggested not only by its appearance but by the sound of *lis*. It is a sad tale of what faulty hearing can do to a beautiful flower and a royal heraldic emblem.

'Gathering Nuts in May'

May is springtime in Britain and therefore the season for sowing and, certainly, not for harvesting. Hence, 'nuts in May' make no sense. In fact, the 'nuts' are misheard 'knots'!

Reference to them goes back to the ancient Roman celebration of May Day. This lasted not just one but six days. Flowers played a significant part in its ritual, which explains the Roman description of the festival as *Floralia.*

When the observance of May Day became universal, the classical practice of gathering *knots* of flowers was continued, to decorate homes, to make posies or, intertwined, to form chains and garlands with which to go 'a-Maying'. Later generations, unacquainted with 'knots', mistook them for 'nuts'. The error was perpetuated by the author of the well-known children's song, 'Here we go gathering nuts in May'.

The Love Apple

Just as love in tennis has no amorous connotation, signifying 'zero', so love apples (an archaic alternate for tomatoes), however tempting their name, were grown in a totally different soil.

Originally, tomatoes were cultivated in South American lands. Introduced into Spain, they reached Italy from Morocco. Italians therefore called the new 'fruit' *pomo dei Moro,* 'the apple of the Moors'. (It must be remembered that in the Middle Ages, Europeans used to apply the name of Moors to all Moslems.) The French, misunderstanding the Italian *pomo dei Moro,* rendered it in their language *pomme d'amour* — 'love apple'!

Erroneously named, it became victim of yet another misconception. Often served with a main course, the tomato was considered a vegetable, though botanically it is a fruit.

The Jew's Harp

Wrong notes offend the musical ear. All the more surprising is the existence of the Jew's harp, the result of mistaking a sound. This small, simple and ancient instrument, in which a single strip of metal held between the teeth, is plucked by a finger, appropriately used to be called a jaw's harp. Misheard, the jaw's harp became the Jew's harp.

A biblical tradition possibly contributed to the misunderstanding and the association of the instrument with Jews. In the well-known story, young David is said to have played the harp so beautifully that its music was able to soothe King Saul's mind during his bouts of melancholia.

Another suggestion traces the Jew's harp to the French 'play trumpet', *jeu tromp*. The English mistook the French *jeu* for 'Jew'. The substitution of the trumpet by a harp is easy to explain. The instrument sounded so much more like it and was equally 'twanged'.

Joss House and Joss Sticks

The Chinese joss is a misunderstood God!

Portuguese travellers, who were among the first Europeans to reach China, were devout Christians. They told the Chinese of their beliefs. To Chinese ears the Portuguese for God — *dios* — sounded like joss, a name possibly arrived at as well by Chinamen's difficulty with pronouncing the Portuguese word properly. This is the (faulty) origin of both the joss house for a Chinese shrine, and joss sticks for their incense.

The Morris Dance

The Morris dance, once a popular English folk dance,

was not called after any individual of that name. Morris is the misheard description of a Moor. Originally, a Moorish military dance, it reached Britain from Spain in the fourteenth century, and the Spanish for Moor is *Morisco*.

There is also a tradition that the 'Moorish' part of its name recalls the custom of those performing the dance to blacken their faces to look like Moors.

'Losing a Ship for a Hap'worth of Tar'

'Losing a ship for a hap'worth of tar', refers to parsimonious people who by saving a little, short-sightedly lose a lot.

Apparently a nautical figure of speech, it is far removed from the sea. It did not speak of a ship at all but — with a rural accent — of a sheep! As a precaution against disease, sheep used to be tarred, an early custom recalled even in Shakespeare's works. To identify their property, sheep owners branded their animals with their initials, doing so with hot tar. To save the small cost, some niggardly farmers trusted luck and did nothing. Consequently, they lost their sheep through sickness or theft.

Not Caring a Fig

Whoever takes the phrase of 'not caring a fig' literally does an injustice to figs. He obviously implies that they are worth very little. This misjudgment is due to a misunderstanding resulting, as it were, from a transplant of the fruit from one culture to another.

This fig of trifling value is uneatable! It is no fig at all, but describes a rude (Spanish and Latin-American) gesture known as *fico*. Made by forming a fist with the thumb protruding between the index and middle fingers, it is meant contemptuously to express the worthlessness of a person or object. Shakespeare used the expression in this sense, when in *Henry V,* he spoke of 'fico for thy friendship' and in *Henry VI,* of 'a fig for Peter'.

Actually, this visual metaphor is not indigenously

Spanish. It can be traced to the ancient Romans, who used it vulgarly as part of their body language to show disdain. Its description as a 'fig', no doubt, was based on the shape made by the hand. Though resembling a fig, its outline also suggested the female genitals! The figurative use of the fig was thus tantamount to telling a person, without uttering a single word, in obscene sexual picture language how much one detested and rejected him.

Nine Tailors Make a Man

Proverbs and sayings have often mystified people, not least so, when they seemed to make little sense. This applies to the observation that 'nine tailors make a man'. In search of a meaning, absurd interpretations have been given. Typical was the suggestion that — at some time — a tailor had so low an opinion of himself that in his own mind he was merely a ninth part of a (real) man!

The saying as it reads now, is the result of a misunderstanding. In former times, when a death occurred in the community, it concerned everyone and not just the immediate family. The passing of a person was therefore publicly announced by the ringing of church bells.

The number of tolls indicated the sex of the deceased. Nine 'tollers' marked a man and six a woman. An alternate word for 'tollers' was 'tellers'. Hence, it could rightly be said that 'nine tellers mark a man'.

With the growth of the population, the practice was eventually discontinued and the phrase became meaningless. No longer understood, it was changed into the absurd statement that 'nine tailors make a man'.

Pumps

Of intriguing origin is the name of pumps. Now worn for comfort and sport, these light, close-fitting shoes once were reserved for formal functions. Worn for 'pomp', the occasion eventually was confused with the footwear which, further corrupted linguistically, assumed the modern form of pumps.

Cinderella's Glass Slipper

Cinderella's glass slipper has become so much part of the fairy tale that to change it in any way would spoil its charm. After all, it was by means of the glass slipper dropped by Cinderella on leaving the ball that the prince who had fallen in love with her, was able to find her again.

However, with a little thought, it becomes apparent that glass slippers fit neither into the story nor on Cinderella's feet! No one would wear them on a cold winter's night. Moreover, to dance in them would prove very difficult.

And, in fact, the earliest French version of the tale does not speak of glass slippers but slippers made of fur, much more in character with the story, the season and the occasion. Comfortable to dance in, fur slippers would keep Cinderella's feet warm in the coldest of nights. They would have been of white ermine, fit for a princess!

The French for 'fur' is *vair* and for 'glass', *verre*. Differently spelled, the two words are almost identical in sound. It was quite easy to mistake one for the other. (It must be remembered that, at the time, stories were mostly not read from a book, but related by word of mouth.) Not magic therefore, but an error changed the fur into glass!

For once the perpetrator of the mistake can be identified. It was the French poet and critic (!) Charles Perrault who in 1697 published the story in a collection of popular fairy tales. He selected it from several versions of 'Cinderella' then in circulation and at his disposal. Each one spoke of a fur slipper which he — erroneously — turned into glass. As all later editions and translations of the fairy tale were based on his text, they copied his mistake, which has never been corrected.

Boots and Saddles

By its very nature — to avoid any delay or misunder-standing — a military command has to be short, to the point and, not least, clear. All the more puzzling and confusing is the old United States cavalry call, 'Boots and

Saddles', summoning soldiers to mount their charges. Its boots are completely out of place. Originally and correctly, it was an order expressed in French, bidding the riders to 'put on the saddle' — *boute celle.* Misunderstood, it became 'boots and saddles'.

'Kiss me, Hardy!'

Generally known and well documented are the last moments of Nelson's life. In his victorious battle against the combined French and Spanish fleets at Trafalgar (21 October 1805), he himself had been mortally wounded. Realizing that he was about to die, he made some last requests to Thomas Hardy, the flag captain and his close friend, who was by his side at the time. He asked Hardy to see to it that his body should not be thrown overboard and made him promise that good care would be taken of Lady Hamilton. He is said to have then expressed the wish, 'Kiss me, Hardy!' and kneeling down, Hardy had kissed the Admiral's cheek. 'Now I'm satisfied,' Nelson said, 'Thank God, I have done my duty!'

It has been suggested that actually Nelson had never made such a request which would have been rather odd, no matter how close their friendship. In the excitement and tension of the situation, the Admiral's words were misunderstood. What Nelson in fact had said was not 'Kiss me, Hardy', but 'Kismet, Hardy!'

This would have been most appropriate. At the very height of his career, Nelson was destined to die and thus was not to savour the glory of his victory, in which once and for all he had shattered Napoleon's dream of naval supremacy. It was all 'Fate' — *Kismet.*

Pumpernickel

Though pumpernickel, the heavy German black bread, originated in the German province of Westphalia (in the seventeenth century), it is claimed that its name is not German. It was so called because of a misheard, and then mispronounced, French observation.

A Frenchman of unknown identity had found the coarse German bread so indigestible that he regarded it unfit for human consumption. All it was good for, he said, was to be fed to his horse — Nicole. So he referred to it as *pain pour Nicole* — 'bread for Nicole'.

Germans liked the sound of the French 'description' of their favourite bread. Not realizing its implication, they adopted it. However, in their accent it sounded like Pumpernickel.

Another version of the same 'etymology' attributes the (French) reference to Napoleon! When he discovered that Nicole, his pet horse, loved the black bread, he requested people to provide it, asking them for *pain pour Nicole*. They not only supplied it, but called it by the emperor's 'demand'.

There is a further 'faultless' derivation of pumpernickel which credits the origin of its name exclusively to the Germans. In calling it so, they made no mistake but were very outspoken and crude. At the time, a common lout was known as a *pumper,* which literally meant a 'stinker'. And did not the coarse bread produce lots of unpleasant wind? The *nickel* part is a later addition. It merely underscored the rather unfortunate side-effect. It stood for 'Old Nick' who — it was claimed — was very partial to this German rye bread, as black as his art. In spite of all his devilish tricks, after having eaten the pumper he could not stop himself suffering from the most malodorous wind. Thus his name was duly added to the 'stinker'. There is also the possibility that people who believed in the devil and all the evil he wrought, attributed the bad smell to him and because of it called the bread 'Nick's stench' — *pumper-nickel.*

Chicken à la King

Chicken may be served in many ways. Obviously, the pride of place should go to chicken à la King.

However, any royal connection of this chicken is

fictitious. No king — ruling or dethroned — was responsible for it. Some say that actually the chicken à la King was conceived in republican America. At the beginning of this century, anxious to please his boss, a Mr E. Clarke King II, the chef of the Brighton Beach Hotel, Long Island, NY, had called the dish after him.

Much more likely is the suggestion that the 'King' was the misheard name of a Mr Keene who patronized the famous Delmonico Restaurant in New York.

Englishmen claim that the chicken was first 'cooked up' in their country. The chef of world-renowned Claridge's, London, was also a keen racing man. He had chosen the name to honour the owner of the prize-winning horse at the Grand Prix in 1881, a Mr J. R. Keene, a regular guest at the establishment.

People have short memories and soon no one — whether in Britain or in the United States — recalled Mr Keene. Chicken à la Keene made no sense. Thus the name was misunderstood and changed into the royal title, for once making ignorance (a culinary) bliss.

The Aitch-bone

A cut of beef from the rump used to provide a comparatively inexpensive meal. No wonder that among the English it became the 'poor man's sirloin'. In the nomenclature of meat cuts, it came to be known as 'aitch-bone', a somewhat puzzling description. How did the letter 'h' find its way there? In fact, its presence is not justified and due only to a confusion of sound. The original 'aitch-bone' was the 'edge-bone'.

Lobster Américaine

That larger fish swallow the smaller ones applies to crustaceans as well, even on menus. Lobster Américaine has nothing American in its distinguishing French sauce or garnish. It comes from Brittany in France, where a region known as Armorica was renowned for its succulent lobsters, which were soon called after it. Its name was too localized, it seemed and, mistaken, shed its Armorican shell to assume the American look.

Perhaps to save the genuineness of the American designation an unsubstantiated tradition has it that because American tourists relished the lobster, it was called by their name. Maybe it was also part of business promotion, cleverly catering to American tastes and patriotism.

Lemon Sole
The lemon sole is a species of plaice or flounder. Its lemon part has been attached to the fish in error. A flat fish, in Old French it was compared with, and actually described as, a 'flat board' (*limande*) which, misheard, was changed into the lemon. Others have discovered in the lemon half of the fish the corrupted Latin root *limus,* for 'mud', and assert that the fish was so called because its usual habitat was deep down in the muddy waters.

Bully Beef
Whatever the taste of bully beef, its name is rather spoilt. The canned meat, indeed, is beef, but its 'bully' part has nothing to do with cattle. It merely tells that the meat is boiled. The bully is all that remains of the French *bouilli* for 'boiled'.

Drunk as Blazes
The fourth-century Armenian Bishop Blaise (or Blazey, as his name is also spelt in some English documents) died as a martyr. Believed to have been tortured with wool-combs before being beheaded, he became the patron saint of woolcombers and was remembered as such annually. Special celebrations were held in his honour. In some places (as in Leicester, England) the commemoration included a great variety of features, such as marches, sporting events, games and, not least, the drinking of plenty of grog. Soon those participating in the fun were identified with the saint and referred to as Blaisers. As not

a few of them were the worse for drink, it was not surprising that people came to describe inebriates as 'drunk as Blaisers'. The comparison became a popular — and well understood — saying far and wide.

With the passing of time, the circumstances and the saint were forgotten and no one knew what the phrase meant. No wonder that eventually it was corrupted into 'as drunk as blazes'.

'Many a Mickle Makes a Muckle'

Although it is generally assumed that the (originally Scottish) proverb 'many a mickle makes a muckle' expressed the obvious fact that many small things add up to much, in its present wording it does not say so. Both 'mickle' and 'muckle' mean 'a lot'. So worded, therefore, the sentence makes no sense, as all it would say is that 'much is much'. Correctly rendered the proverb said 'Many a little (or pickle) makes a mickle'. This is yet another example how one misheard word can lead to much confusion.

Rotten Row

'Rotten Row' is an awful name for the beautiful shady track horseriders have been enjoying for so many years in London's Hyde Park. Who could have suggested such an ugly description? In fact, no one ever did. There never was a 'Rotten Row'. Majestically, it was called a 'Royal route' as the King and Queen used to take it whenever they travelled from the palace at Westminster to the forest. At the time, French was the language of courtiers who therefore referred to this 'Kings' way as *route du roi*. Ordinary citizens, unacquainted with court French, misinterpreted what they heard. To their English ears it sounded very much like Rotten Row. Their (corrupted) description thus survives as a relic from the distant past.

Auburn

A person's hair colour might not always be the original

one. Individual taste, fads and modern dyes may be the root-cause of the change. However, long before people ever thought of altering what nature had given them, error achieved the same — playing the trick by a simple mix-up.

It happened in the case of very fair-haired people. Their hair looked 'rather white', *alburnus* in the original Latin. (The word is related to *albus* for 'white', which is still present in the albino and even in the 'white' of an egg, the albumen.)

Romans thus called a fair-haired person *alburnus,* a description which was adopted in Old French as *alborne,* sometimes pronounced abron. The word then struck trouble. To English ears it sounded very much like their own 'brown', *broune* at the time, and soon the two colours were mixed (up). Misunderstanding what was being said, many people erroneously believed that 'auburn' (the ultimate form of the new word) was not 'rather white' but (reddish) brown! What modern chemistry still cannot do, incorrect hearing had achieved, at least linguistically: to dye hair permanently!

Famous Taverns
English taverns, indeed, are unique. Not a few of their names are truly delightful, if not bizarre. Some of the oddest are the result of plain misunderstanding, an error in hearing!

The Bag of Nails
To be called 'The Bag of Nails' seems a peculiar choice of name for an inn. It has been linked with the early period, when nails were still handmade and hence costly. Nail makers who favoured this specific 'pub', it is said, used to pay for their drinks not in cash but in kind — with a bag of nails. Their method of settling accounts took people's fancy, who soon identified the inn with its special customers and their 'bag of nails'.

The story, however plausible, is far from the truth. The

original (and real) name of the inn was 'The Bacchanals', the English rendering of Bacchanalia. This was a Roman feast celebrated in honour of Bacchus, the god of wine, with plenty of drink! When the Romans invaded Britain, they brought with them the practice. Its exuberant drinking bouts were remembered long after the Romans' departure and nostalgically led to the use of the Bacchanals as a favourite name for inns.

To the general public, enjoying their pints, Bacchanals, of course, meant nothing. So they misunderstood the word and, interpreting it their way, believed that it spoke of a 'bag of nails'. This became the accepted version, now even depicted on the inn-sign.

The Ship Inn

A 'Ship Inn' situated at the seaside would be a welcome invitation to sailors. But to find a tavern of that name away from the sea, in a Cheshire village (at Styal), has rightly made people wonder. Could it not be compared with the existence of an admiralty in land-logged Switzerland? Its name, too, is the result of mishearing. In the dialect of the region shippen or shippon was a cowshed and that was originally the tavern's name. Cowsheds, certainly, were plentiful in that part of the country, and for an inn to be so called was most appropriate.

The Cat and Fiddle

Some public houses are known as 'The Cat and Fiddle' and, accordingly, display on their signpost a cat playing the violin. The strange combination is due to a misunderstanding, going back to an historic encounter.

Caton is said to have been a Knight of renown who had distinguished himself at Calais. In recognition of his bravery, he was dubbed *Caton le Fidèle* — 'Caton, the Faithful'. To honour him, the British called an inn in his (French) name. Fame is fickle and French to most of the English, a foreign tongue. *Caton le Fidèle* thus sounded to them like a 'Cat and Fiddle'.

The Pig and Whistle

If cats are supposed to play the fiddle, it seems not so absurd either for pigs to whistle, at least in the name of taverns in which, after having downed a number of drinks, patrons might imagine lots of things. And yet, 'The Pig and Whistle' is not the creation of fable or intoxicated minds. The name, too, belongs to the world of intriguing misunderstandings and has been traced back to completely diverse situations.

Piggen was the Old Saxon word for the 'pail', in which beer was served in the early days, for the guest to dip in his mug. The mug was known by the diminutive of piggen, as *pig. Wassail,* on the other hand, expressed the Anglo-Saxon wish 'Be well!' and 'Be of good health!' — *Was hael.*

Piggen Wassail as the name of an inn, thus invited passers-by to partake of its pails of ale to gain good health! When no longer understood, *Piggen Wassail* was thought to represent a Pig and Whistle.

Others have discovered in the Pig and Whistle a corruption of words from the Anglo-Saxon version of the Gospels: 'Pige-Washail', the angel Gabriel's Salutation to the Virgin Mary, as it appears in the Gospel of St Luke (1:28), 'Hail, thou that art highly favoured ...'

Another, mundane explanation belongs to Shakespeare's time. A servant, when asked to fetch a *pig* of ale, was not trusted. To prevent him from taking a swig 'on the way', he was asked to whistle. Certainly, this made it impossible for him to wet his whistle!

The Swan With Two Necks

No one would ever forget a 'swan with two necks' or a tavern so called. Nevertheless, it was not good advertising or a freak bird that created the name.

Swans once were the exclusive property of the British Crown. They were indeed royal birds. In the fifteenth century, however, English kings introduced the practice to present some of their swans to people they favoured, and to own such royally donated birds came to be regarded a privilege. Among the recipients so honoured were the Dyers and Vintners, at the time two of the most powerful Guilds.

A problem soon arose. As all swans looked alike, it was difficult to determine whose property they were. Eventually, an easy method was devised to tell the difference. Annually, during the third week of July, three 'swan masters' (representing the Crown and the two Guilds) caught and examined every bird on the river Thames, a custom which became known as 'swan upping'. The swans allotted to the Vintners were 'branded' by two *nicks* in their beaks.

It was not surprising that Vintners who owned such swans were justly proud of the fact. If they also ran an inn, as many of them did at the time, they publicized their privilege by calling it 'The Swan with the Two Nicks'. When ultimately, the custom was forgotten, people had no idea what a swan with two nicks meant. Thus the — misheard — 'swan with two necks' was hatched.

A Parting Shot

All things come to an end, though wits have observed that a sausage has two. Mistakes, however, seem never to cease. Even a 'parting shot' is not what it sounds like to our ears. It is completely foreign indeed and was last heard ages ago.

The ancient Parthians, who lived south-east of the Caspian Sea, had a strange war-practice. The moment their mounted archers had shot off their arrows they turned their horses around as if to flee to mislead the enemy. The deceptive manoeuvre became known as 'the Parthian shot'. When the Parthians had disappeared from the historical scene, those ignorant of their former existence and name mistook the Parthian shot as a parting shot.

3 Optical Illusions — Things Are Not What They Appear

It is told of a wise man in the East that, in his daily prayer, he asked for the gift to see today with the eyes of tomorrow. In many of our concepts and figures of speech we continue to do the opposite. In spite of evidence to the contrary, we perpetuate optical illusions of yesteryear. Numerous indeed are the visual fallacies which we have never discarded. After all, we still speak of the rising and setting sun.

Fata Morgana

The most famous of all optical illusions — observed from antiquity to our own days — is the Fata Morgana. We see something that is not there. Scientifically, the phenomenon has been explained as the result of irregular reflection and refraction of light rays passing through layers of air of varied density and temperature. Its description as Fata Morgana goes back to Arthurian legend and mirages that occurred in southern Italy, in the Strait of Messina. Nearby in Calabria — just across the water — so myth believed, was the home of the Fairy Morgan (*Fata Morgana* in Italian), half-sister of King Arthur. The miraculous mirage of the fabulous city, seen by an eighteenth-century Dominican friar, was attributed to her sorcery and became known by her name. A figure of fable thus lives on in every mirage we see.

Blue-Blooded

To describe members of the aristocracy as blue-blooded

is not a mere colourful figure of speech, but based on historical circumstances and yet another optical illusion. It goes back to medieval times, when Spanish noblemen looked down on the Moorish invaders and their descendants. The two races differed in the pigmentation of their skin. This made the blue veins on the hands and forehead of the indigenous, fair-skinned Spaniards stand out conspicuously, whilst the blood vessels of identical colour hardly showed up on the swarthy North African Moors. Prompted by racial prejudice, the haughty Spanish noblemen actually believed that the colour of their blood differed and that God, in selecting them, had indicated their superior status by filling their veins with blue blood! The optical illusion was never corrected and, as a linguistic monument of early discrimination, created a peculiarly tainted nobility.

Drink Like a Fish

To say of anyone intemperate that he drinks like a fish, is based on an optical illusion. In fact, if taken literally, it would mean that he is drinking very little indeed. Because fish appear constantly to be swallowing water, it only seems that they are drinking it. In reality, the water never enters their stomach. It passes through their gills which extract from it necessary oxygen. Any liquid the fish require is absorbed from their food.

Monkeys and Fleas

The antics of monkeys amuse grown-ups as much as children. Watching the animals search each other's fur and then, with apparent delight, swallow whatever they have found, led to the mistaken belief that — in mutual aid — they were defleaing each other.

What they actually do is not to pick fleas from their fellow's hairy coat, but to remove dandruff and loose pieces of dead skin! Their activity is prompted not by any desire to groom each other or to rid themselves of irritating vermin. The skin and dandruff contains a salty substance essential for the animals' diet and hence is relished by them. The practice therefore serves their own well-being and pleasure and has nothing to do with flea-hunting.

Monkey's Face

It is a mistake to apply human concepts to the animal world, not least so to the facial expression of the great apes. Their mien might convey a totally different attitude to what the identical features would indicate in man. When, for instance, a chimpanzee is highly elated, it 'looks' angry. On the other hand, its apparently funny face does not display amusement but in most cases is a contortion of anger or pain.

The Camel's Hoofs

Even the Bible contains not only a striking example of wrong observation, but legislated accordingly. To protect the feet of the camel from the hot desert sand, nature provided them with pads. They cover up the animal's cloven hoofs, which thus cannot be seen at a glance. This led the ancient Hebrews to imagine that the camel, though chewing the cud, did not fulfil the second essential qualification for being counted among the 'clean' animals which would make its flesh 'fit' (*kasher*) for consumption — having split hoofs. Consequently, the Bible (erroneously) included camel meat in the list of forbidden foods. It is a case in which not seeing things properly proved (for the camel) a lifesaver!

The Bald Eagle

Several reasons made Americans adopt the bald eagle as their national emblem. A majestic bird, it symbolized strength. Early colonists took special note of a feature that distinguished it from the eagle they knew 'back home'. However, in identifying it, they committed an error, which they perpetuated in its name. The eagle is white-headed and not bald!

Suntan

Looks can deceive. Suntan is generally assumed to promote and reflect good health. This is far from the truth. In fact, to expose the bare skin too much to the ultraviolet rays of the sun, able to penetrate even thick cloud-cover, can prove dangerous. The tanning effect of 'sun-bathing' is not a sign of well-being, but nature's attempt to protect the skin from suffering harmful damage.

Sun Shining on Fire

An optical illusion led people to imagine that if the sun shone on a fire, it extinguished it. This is not so. The fallacious impression arose from the fact that the brightness of the sun made the glowing embers almost invisible.

There is another possibility that might have given rise to the fallacy. On a cold and cloudy winter's day, the flames of a fire are a very noticeable source of warmth and to keep the fire going more fuel is added. However, when on occasions the sun suddenly broke through the cloud-cover, its warmth made people forget to stoke the fire, with the result that it died. Not realizing the cause, they thought that the sun had put out the flames.

Twinkling Stars

Stars do not twinkle. They only appear to do so. The optical illusion is the effect of the atmosphere through which the light reflected from the stars passes on its way to earth. Ann Taylor's well-known rhyme, 'Twinkle, twinkle, little star', certainly did its part to perpetuate the wrong interpretation of the phenomenon.

Vanishing Stars

For thousands of years man believed that the stars vanished from the sky during the day. Not seeing them, he reasoned that, with the arrival of dawn, they must have moved away, to return again at nightfall. He did not realize that the brightness of the sky, lit up by the 'risen' sun, made the stars merely invisible to his eyes.

Canals on Mars

Modern space research has destroyed the long-held 'view' of the existence of artificially-created canals on Mars. The pictures taken by *Mariner IV* in 1964, and subsequent probes, proved and confirmed the fallacy of the sensational claim. The canals 'seen', did not exist.

When (in 1877) the Italian astronomer Giovanni Schiaparelli first observed fissures and rifts on the red planet, he was greatly intrigued and his imagination fired. Their regular pattern and straightness suggested to him that only intelligent (Martian) beings could have designed and constructed them. He named them *canali,* 'channels'. A rather ambiguous term, it was subject to various interpretations. Translated into English, it was rendered 'canals'. This led to the assumption that they were 'waterways'. It has been conjectured that the optical illusion, not least, was the result of a defect in the human eye.

4 Clerical Errors and Misprints

During the Dark Ages not only the ordinary man and woman, but also those in highest office, could neither read nor write. If their signature was needed, they made a simple cross. Literacy was confined to members of certain clerical orders. Monks and priests thus were called upon to draw up legal documents and write personal letters. Eventually, ecclesiastics lost their unique status and others were able to take their place, but the 'clerical' past of scribes (and accountants) was never forgotten. It survives in the (slightly contracted) name of the clerk which still carries within it its religious root.

However conscientious and learned a person may be, he is bound to make a mistake here and there. No one is infallible and, at times, there is a human tendency to get things wrong. That is why authors proofread and even the latest models of electronic typewriters provide an ingenious correcting device.

In most cases, mistakes were recognized and duly rectified. Through the years it also happened that they slipped by unnoticed and, once made, were adopted and have become an integral part of a people's culture. Indeed, clerical errors that have been perpetuated, make up an impressive list.

In the Beginning God Created Water and Earth

A copyist's error concerning one letter may well have become part of the creation story at the very beginning of the Bible, introducing into it a perplexing inconsistency. That this is rarely noticed shows how something too well known might become so familiar that we take it for granted, and fail to observe the most obvious.

According to the text as it now stands, 'In the beginning God created *heaven* and earth.' The earth was without form and void and the spirit of God 'hovered over the face of the waters'. On the second day God divided the waters by a firmament which he called *heaven* ...

Anyone reading this account for the first time as if it were an ordinary story, would immediately be struck by an incongruity. Where did the waters come from, which God divided on the second day? There is no mention of their creation. On the other hand, heaven comes into existence twice, both on the first day and on the second day. It just does not make sense.

A clerical error could be the simplest explanation, resolving the difficulty. The ancient Hebrew in which the Bible was written had no space between the words, nor any vowels. Each line presented a continuous row of consonants and only the learned were able to read the text correctly, knowing where to divide the words and which vowels to add. The Hebrew for 'water' is *MAYIM* and for 'heaven', *SHAMAYIM*. In the original method of writing the two words (MYM and SHMYM) differed by a single letter: the added 'sh' of the heaven. Moreover, the two consonants — the *mem* and the *shin* — looked so similar that they could easily be confused. The original text might well have read, 'In the beginning God created water and earth.' The rest would then follow on logically. He subsequently divided the waters by a firmament which he called heaven.

A simple writing mistake on the part of a copyist thus rendered an essential part of the creation story unintelligible. Water and earth are well known as the primal elements in many cosmogenies.

The Wicked Bible

The 'Wicked Bible' was published in London in 1631 and truly merited its disparaging name. It was bestowed on it because of the omission of one single word! Containing the complete text of Holy Scripture, it lacks the 'NOT' in the Seventh Commandment (Ex. 20:14). This therefore declared that 'Thou shalt commit adultery'.

It is easy to imagine the consternation the faulty Bible created. Archbishop Dr William Laud immediately ordered all copies to be confiscated and to be destroyed. The printers, who blamed an anonymous typesetter for the error, were fined £3,000. It was a considerable sum then which, in fact, ruined their business. (To make things worse, they were Robert Barker and Martin Lucas of Blackfriars, the king's printers!)

A small number of the 1,000 copies printed of this 'Wicked Bible', (which also became known as the 'Adulterous Bible') escaped the purge. They are now highly prized collectors' items.

Whitsun

The Christian feast of Pentecost (from the Greek word for '50th') is so called because it is celebrated fifty days after Easter. It commemorates the descent of the Holy Spirit on the Apostles, said to have taken place on that day. Anglican churches do not call it Pentecost but Whitsun. It is a puzzling name because of the (literal) loss of a letter and a day. Converts used to be baptized on this seventh Sunday after Easter and wore white robes for the ceremony. This made the English refer to the day as White Sunday. The tradition lapsed and the name of the feast contracted into Whitsun, a now meaningless word — lacking the 'e' of white and the 'day' of Sunday.

Conjugal Rights

Conjugal rights are now taken to speak specifically of the mutual obligation of a husband and wife — mostly in a sexual sense. This, however, is the result of a misspelling.

Originally, the term referred to the *rites* of the Church. Not a slip of the tongue, but a clerical error changed a religious ceremony that wedded a man and a woman into a legal 'affair'.

LBS — The Wrong Weight

To use 'lbs' as an abbreviation for 'pounds' of weight is an error. Obviously, the letters are meant to be a contraction of the Latin for 'pounds', *librae,* which lacks the 's'. This was added mistakenly from the English. Correctly shortened the (Latin) 'pounds' should appear as 'lb'.

The Nickname

A nickname in itself is not real. It is the result of a misunderstanding, of a wrong kind of separation or attachment — whichever way it is looked upon. All the term intended to convey was that it was an 'additional' name, an 'also'-name, which Middle English expressed as 'an *eke*-name'. Somehow the final 'n' of the 'an' lost its proper position and, changing sides, made eke-name a neke-name, eventually to be pronounced and written nickname.

The Thorn in the Alphabet

Most people mispronounce 'Ye' whenever they see it in supposedly Old English names, as 'Ye Olde Coffee Shoppe'. They make it sound like *yee,* as if it were the archaic form of the plural for 'you' (ye), still used in the Authorized Version of the Bible. This is quite incorrect. The 'Ye' should be pronounced as *the,* because the 'Y' is not a 'Y' in this case. The confusion arose through an early clerical error!

Our present-day alphabet has evolved from an earlier one and lacks an important letter, once part of it and fulfilling a very useful role. Known in runic as 'thorn', it represented our present-day 'th'-sound, so frequent on the Anglo-Saxon tongue.

With the passing of time, the thorn's shape

deteriorated and, incorrectly transcribed, came to look very much like the 'Y'. This made printers, lacking the character of the thorn in their font, use the 'Y' in its stead. As the letter now served two totally different sounds, inevitably these were mixed up.

Sidney or Sydney

People observe meticulously the difference of spelling between Sidney and Sydney. They imagine that it must have some fundamental reason or meaning. There is none in fact. Written either way, both Sidney and Sydney originated from the contraction of a third-century French saint's name — St Dennis. The variation developed in the early days of the printing press, when typesetters frequently interchanged the 'i' and the 'y'.

The Syllabus

A syllabus sets out a course of studies, listing the subjects to be taught. It is all the more unfortunate that the term was victim of a mistake and in both its present-day spelling and meaning combines a misprint and a wrong deduction.

Cicero (106–43 B.C.) was not only a Roman statesman of renown, an orator and philosopher, but also a man of letters, in every sense of the word. More than 800 of his letters are preserved, covering a period of twenty-six years. In one of his 'Letters to Atticus' he refers to *sittybas,* the Greek description for the parchment strips or labels which used to be attached to the scrolls (the precursor of books), giving their title and author. The 1470 publication of these letters misspelled the term as syllabus. The error was never corrected but copied in all later editions. That is how the modern syllabus came into existence. Scholars unaware of the reason, wondered what the etymological root of the word was. In their search for it they wrongly traced it to a Greek expression that spoke of something which was 'put together'. Thus they added another mistake, now perpetuated in the modern meaning of syllabus which therefore, and very literally so, was born in error.

Wisteria

The wisteria misspells the name of the very person it is meant to honour: nineteenth-century American anatomist Caspar Wistar, who was the first to discover the flower.

In 1818, the very year of Wistar's death at the early age of fifty-seven, Thomas Nuttal, the curator of the Botanical Gardens at Harvard, decided to call the plant after him. Careless in the spelling of the name, he rendered it wisteria. All later attempts at correcting the mistake and recall in the flower the professor's name rightly spelled — as wistaria — failed.

The Harebell

The hare in the harebell is out of place. Its presence is due to a mistake.

The plant's bell-shaped flowers are suspended from stalks of almost *hair*-like thinness. This made botanists name the wild hyacinth (also known as the bluebell of Scotland) a hairbell. Misunderstood, the hair was interpreted as a hare.

Mayonnaise

However well-prepared, mayonnaise lacks one ingredient — the proper spelling of its name. Opinions differ, as to what it ought to be. All agree that the clerical error covers up significant data.

Generally it is believed that mayonnaise was called after Port Mahon, the capital city of the island of Minorca in the western Mediterranean Sea.

The British who had captured the island during the Spanish War of Succession, were finally driven out by the French (in 1756). To celebrate the victory and make Frenchmen recall it at (many of) their meals — with relish so it is said, mayonnaise was created!

This explanation seemed unsatisfactory. People felt that there had to be some additional reason for the choice of the special dressing. This gave rise to a story told about the Duc de Richelieu, who had led the victorious French forces. Always fond of food, he was ravenous after the battle, but he looked in vain for something to eat. The army kitchen had used up all rations. To satisfy their general, the cooks occupied the nearest home and in its kitchen tossed into a bowl whatever food they could find in the larder. The meal they then prepared surpassed anything Richelieu had ever tasted.

When the story eventually reached Paris, it became the talk of the town. A French chef hearing it, immediately spied his chance. Without losing a moment, he set about to contrive a new dressing, made up of ingredients that would delight a gourmet. Appealing to French patriotism, he named his new creamy sauce mahonnaise, in honour of the French victory at Port Mahon, hoping thereby to ensure its instant adoption.

A war monument in the form of a relish which has outlived many other memorials built of rock and stone, in itself is unique in the annals of history. Even odder would be the phenomenon that, in memory of a (long-forgotten) victory of one people, all nations, including the defeated British, continue to enjoy a dressing called after the site of battle.

The city of Bayonne (in south-west France) refused to accept the bellicose origin of the sauce. Already famous for its hams, woollens and soap, it sought the credit for the invention of mayonnaise as well. Its citizens therefore asserted that, correctly spelled, this should be known as bayonnaise!

Irishmen begged to differ. They registered their own claim, saying that mayonnaise had come from their country. It had been called after General MacMahon, one of their great soldiers, whose chef had concocted the dressing in his honour. Hence, it should rightly be called MacMahonnaise.

There are other explanations, all based on some mis-spelling. The name mayonnaise, it was claimed, was meant to make reference to the many egg yolks used in preparing it. Hence it should be described as *moyeunaise*.

Antonin Carême, the French chef of the future King George IV, suggested yet another etymology. Mayonnaise was derived from the French for to 'stir' (*manier*) as, certainly, the sauce would lack perfection unless properly 'stirred'.

The Admiral

Even those of highest rank are not exempt from error. This applies to an Admiral as well. His title, of Arab stock, contains a letter which does not belong there and, altogether, is jumbled.

A Moslem ruler, prince or commander is known as Amir or Emir. Arabs thus referred (at least as early as the twelfth century) to those in charge of their Mediterranean navy as *Amir-al-bahr* — 'ruler of the sea'. Crusaders possibly brought the title to Europe, where it was finally adopted by the British. Though a maritime nation, they strangely dropped the 'sea' (*bahr*), so that all that was left was Amir-al. Ignorant of Arabic, they further confused the already truncated name with the Latin for 'admirable', resulting in the Admiral.

Later generations tried to rationalize the error. They explained that, as a seafaring people, the British admired their navy and wanted to pay special respect to its chief. This led them to imagine that the description of his rank was not derived from the Moslems but expressed (from Roman roots) all that was 'admirable'.

The Navvy

Men, first employed to build the canals criss-crossing Britain, were nicknamed navvies. It was the shortened form of their original description as navigators, a name given to them as, to begin with, the canals were known as 'navigations'.

The construction of the 365 miles (550 kilometres) of canals was supervised by James Brindley (1716–72), a prominent engineer. A real expert in his profession, he used neither written calculations nor drawings. A self-taught man, his spelling left much room for improvement. Whenever writing of his labourers, he misspelled their name as navvy-gators. Doing heavy work, they liked to quench their thirst with lots of drink. Rather rough fellows with uncouth manners, people came to fear them. All that is left now of those pioneer '*navi*gators' is the navvy, a remnant of a significant chapter in the history of English communications and a famous engineer's illiteracy.

The Sentry

A sentry is a soldier on guard whose designation shields an early error which was responsible for several mis-interpretations of his title. These include the false claim that the 'sentry' was derived from the sentinel, or the (French) 'path' — *sentier* — he covered in the course of his duty or patrols. Equally unlikely is the further suggestion that 'sentry' was a colloquial contraction of a former 'sanctuary'. As a place of safety, it had served watchmen as a shelter.

What really happened was an unfortunate exchange of its initial letter. This, originally, was not an 's' but a 'c'. The sentry's office goes back to the military organization of ancient Rome which included heavy infantry groups, each counting a hundred men and therefore known as 'centuries'. The officers commanding them accordingly were known as 'centurions'. Following this tradition, the 'private' in the English army (still in the eighteenth century) used to be referred to as a 'private centinnel'.

Tweed

The rough, hard-wearing cloth known as tweed, is not named after the river Tweed, though it was first manu-factured in Scotland. A clerical error and not a geographical feature is woven into (the name of) the material. Its original description was not tweed at all, but 'tweel', the Scottish for 'twill', recalling the manner in which it was made. Unfamiliar with the Gaelic tongue, people came to assume that not tweel, but tweed was the correct name of the fabric.

Gossip

Gossip is the result of a close relationship. Few would suspect God's presence in such idle talk. But that is how all gossip started. The word is a misspelling of God-sib, the ancient Saxon for a 'kinsman of God'. This was the name given to whoever acted as the sponsor of a child at baptism. (The God-sib developed into the modern Godparent.)

Eventually, the range of those described as God-sib was extended to include near relatives and intimate friends. When meeting, it was only human for them to discuss other people and their affairs (of any kind), with the result that their name, now corrupted into gossip, became synonymous with tittle-tattle.

It's All Boloney

Foolishness may be the result of many causes, which certainly applies to — the American-born — boloney. This colloquial description of nonsensical and foolish talk has been derived from a multitude of sources: the (corrupted) name of a city, a music hall, the political platform and the slaughterhouse — a mixed bag indeed.

It has been said that the (silly) boloney (or, baloney, as mostly used nowadays) came from the Italian city of Bologna — misspelled and mispronounced. Why, of all places, this town should have been chosen to be so abused, seems rather puzzling. Far from being a centre of unreason, Bologna was the site of the oldest European university, founded in 1088.

Nevertheless, the claim may be correct, as boloney did not refer to any of the city's inhabitants, but to a large sausage, either produced there, or named after it by Italian migrants to the United States. No one knew for sure its ingredients. They could be of the most inferior (and nauseating) kind, and to those who did not fancy the sausage, 'boloney' became synonymous with anything of dubious origin and taste. Dislike and misspelling may thus have been responsible for the first boloney.

Another version moves the birthplace of boloney to the Chicago stockyards, where butchers are said to have launched it. When they thought that the meat of an old bull was too tough, they remarked that it was fit only for the making of a sausage, the bologna. The word soon deteriorated into the 'unfit' boloney.

Others have found nothing corrupt in boloney. They 'explained' that Jack Convey (d. 1928), an ex-baseball player turned actor, had invented the word on the spur of the moment during a vaudeville show. His 'silly' improvisation had caught on, perhaps helped by the fact that he also wrote for *Variety,* the theatrical weekly, widely-read throughout the States.

Politicians are fond of making memorable remarks. The Hon. Alfred E. ('Al') Smith has been credited with having popularized (though not originated) in 1934 all that is 'boloney'. Condemning the proposed introduction of new dollar coins, the gold content of which was to be greatly reduced, he contemptuously referred to them as 'boloney dollars'. And a politician's words are well publicized.

Totally different is yet another derivation that traces boloney to the gypsy tongue and its mispronounced description of testicles, *pelone.* In fact, it was all 'balls'.

Double Talk

Some people repeat themselves, saying things all over again, though they might do so with different words. We decry such repetition as a waste of time and as boring. We do not realize that, frequently and without knowing it, we ourselves commit the same offence. It has become an integral part of ordinary speech, technically known as tautology, from the Greek *tauto* for 'the same' and *logo* for 'saying'.

The phenomenon has a valid reason. Language, like everything that lives, changes. Words and expressions that once were part of everyday speech, age and become obsolete. However, instead of replacing the archaic term with its modern synonym, possibly introduced from abroad, language adds the one to the other, thereby duplicating whatever is being said. Numerous examples can be found in almost every aspect of life.

The Salt Cellar

When at the dinner table we ask for the 'salt cellar', we say salt twice over. This cellar has nothing to do with the basement but is the French version of the Latin for 'salt'. We merely repeat in French what has already been said in English. Americans have eliminated the error by doing away with the salt cellar and putting the salt shaker in its place.

The Turnip

'Neap'—the Old English word for 'round'—was the descriptive name given to the common vegetable which served cattle, sheep and men as a nourishing staple food. By the sixteenth century people must have forgotten its meaning, because they preceded the 'neap' by the French *tour,* equally referring to the root's 'roundness'. This created our turnip (a contraction of the *tour* and the *neap*), which is thus round twice over, as it were a double circle.

Reindeer

Not only children might imagine that reindeer were so called because of the reins held by Father Christmas to direct the animals drawing his legendary sledge. In fact, the second part of the animal's name merely echoes the first, which is the Old Norse word for 'deer'.

The Hoi Polloi

Those who condescendingly speak of 'the common crowd' as 'the hoi polloi' give away their own ignorance. A Greek expression, *hoi* represents the definite article. *Hoi polloi* already means 'the many' and hence to speak of 'the hoi polloi' literally doubles up the article, saying 'the the many'.

The Sahara Desert

A desert is assumed to be an arid region in which little grows. And yet, those speaking of the 'Sahara Desert' — unknowingly — have given it a gift of growth, actually doubling it up. Sahara, from the Arabic *sahr,* already means a 'desert'.

The Mistletoe

Those kissing under the mistletoe may wonder why this parasitic plant is renowned for its magic qualities. Its name certainly lacks all logic. The 'toe' at its end (from the Old English *tan* for 'twig') merely reiterates the foregoing 'mistle', which in reality therefore is redundant.

Misprints

Printers' errors are a fascinating study in themselves. However efficient a typesetter may be, they are bound to occur. It is no wonder that proof galleys leave ample room for corrections —

Reviewing a book by a prominent historian, a scholarly magazine praised it as a 'provocative contribution from a well-known shitorian'.

When a president of France, renowned for his tallness, strongly supported a proposition, a newspaper report stated that he 'threw his *h*eight behind the plan'. After all, *w*eight and height may be correlated!

A plain of land described by an author as being widely covered with 'erratic blocks' was made to be strewn with 'erotic blacks'.

An obituary notice for a beloved and 'dear' father was

made to read, 'In loving memory of a very dead Dad.'

There are unfortunate misprints. Much indignation followed a newspaper report during the First World War which, quoting one of the then Prime Minister's speeches, had him say that 'Everything is ready, even the coffins for the troops.' The offending word, of course, was meant to read 'coffee'.

Fritz Spiegl in 'A collection of clangers, misprints and other typographical disasters' (*What the Papers Didn't Mean to Say*, Scouse Press, Liverpool) quotes a striking example of how the omission of a single letter might create havoc, if not a diplomatic incident. A State dinner had 'harmoniously' brought together the American and Russian leaders. Subsequently it was reported that at the conclusion of the meal, when Mr Khrushchev led Mrs Eisenhower by the arm down the Embassy steps, 'President Eisenhower took Mrs Khrushchev's ars.' To make things worse, the account continued to relate that, on the occasion, 'the Soviet Prime Minister was smiling broadly and obviously enjoying himself'.

A personal example may serve as a final illustration. In my book on Judaism, *The Star of David*, I explain the unique Jewish institution of a religious quorum. This stipulates that for a public service to be held, the presence of a minimum number of ten adult males is required. Democratically, tradition stressed that their standing in the community did not matter. Everyone counted equally. In support, I quoted an ancient rabbinical adage to this effect which said, 'Ten shoemakers make a quorum but nine rabbis don't.' On reading the proofs, I discovered that a printer's error had changed the saying to read that 'Ten shoemakers make a quorum but nine rabbits don't!' I was very tempted not to correct the mistake but instead to add a footnote to the rabbits, saying, 'Not yet, but very soon!'

At times a misprint, indeed, can express the truth more subtly than the intended version.

5 Sailing Under False Colours

Not to attract undue attention prior to their attacking a ship, pirate vessels would fly the flag of a friendly nation, thus 'sailing under false colours'. This is the origin of the phrase.

Figuratively speaking, modern civilization has adopted numerous concepts and traditions equally misleading and deceptive. It shows how a mistake, once made, sticks and, apparently irresistible and irreversible, choughtlessly is transmitted from one generation to another.

Colourblindness
It is a mistake to speak of colourblindness. The description suggests that people suffering from this defect cannot recognize any colour, their visual world being altogether grey, which is exceedingly rare. In the majority of cases, those afflicted with colourblindness cannot differentiate between certain colours, mostly red and/or green while all others can be distinguished by them, only less vividly.

Rembrandt's 'Nightwatch'
A landmark in Rembrandt's paintings is his famous (1642) group portrait, known worldwide as *The Nightwatch*. The title was never his and is a misnomer. The picture does not show guardsmen but members of a citizens' shooting club. They are not on watch nor is it night! For 150 years the painting was known correctly as

The Company of Frans Banning Cocq. Rembrandt depicted the men as leaving an armoury — at noon — either to go on parade or to a shooting contest.

The erroneous name was given to the painting only towards the end of the eighteenth century. For many years it had been displayed in the Amsterdam Town Hall, which was heated in winter by a large peat fire. No doubt, the smoke of the peat covered the picture with a layer of soot, creating the wrong impression of watchmen at night. Custodians, concerned to preserve the precious painting, decided to protect it with a (further) layer of varnish. This, at the time, was slightly tinted with caramel, thereby adding to the darkness and gloom of the picture. No one therefore came to question the authenticity of the *Nightwatch* title, in reality so anachronistic and incorrect.

The Olympic Gold Medal

Olympic 'gold medals' are not of gold. Priceless to the winner in symbolic value, the gold in their name is not solid. It refers merely to the thin plating that covers the medal, of which nine-tenths is silver.

Rosewood and Dogwood

In spite of its name, rosewood has no botanical link with the rose. The hard, dark timber of leguminous trees owes the misleading description to its faint roselike odour. A similar reason explains the name of the American dogwood. It is so called not because dogs favour it, but because it is said to smell like a wet dog.

Nuts Not Nutty

Nuts — so hard to crack — have given many a problem. As their shape somewhat reminded people of that of a head, the nut became its slang name. In spite of their hard shell, some nuts were found to have deteriorated inside, which led to the description of the mentally sick as 'nutty'. There is nothing nutty, however, in the walnut. Like cashews and almonds, it is not a nut, but belongs to the species of fruit known as drupe, of which peaches and olives are other members.

French Beans

Though France has been the master of cuisine, French beans do not come from there. Their home is Latin America.

The Jerusalem Artichoke

The Jerusalem artichoke is indigenous to Peru. Italians introduced it into Europe. As its stems and leaves seemed to resemble those of the sunflower, they called it the 'sunflower artichoke', *girasole articiocco*. The choice of *girasole* referred to the plant's 'turning towards the sun'.

People ignorant of Italian, misunderstood *girasole* for Jerusalem, a name certainly so much better known and remembered than an Italian foreign word. More so, a vegetable linked with the Holy City would ensure its popularity, and hence its sale!

The Panama Hat

Panama hats originated in Ecuador, Panama's southern neighbour. The misleading use of the Central American republic's name was due to the fact that Panama used to be the chief exporter of the hat, which in the beginning was hand-plaited from the leaves of the scew-pine.

The Turkish Bath

The Turkish bath is neither a bath nor Turkish. However, because it was introduced into Europe from the Middle East at the time when the Turkish Ottoman Empire dominated that entire region, it was regarded 'Turkish'. In Turkey itself, it was known as *Hamman,* an Arab word recalling the 'heat' generated by the steam which induced copious perspiration.

Its prototype was a very similar kind of bath, already known to the Romans. They treated the body with a sequence of sweating, cold baths and oiling of the skin.

Gypsies

Through the centuries, gypsies have been among the most maligned and rejected of people. Shunned and hunted from one place to another, theirs has been a homeless existence. In spite of it, they faithfully maintained their own culture and traditions.

Their real home was the north-west of India, where they lived as members of a low caste. They left India between the twelfth and fifteenth centuries, to migrate to the west. It was eventually from Egypt that they reached northern European countries where they were therefore mistaken for Egyptians and so called. But usage (or contempt) made people corrupt their Egyptian description which survives fragmentally as gypsies.

Gypsy Music

What is generally enjoyed and described as gypsy music is Hungarian.

The Pennsylvania Dutch

The Pennsylvania Dutch are not Dutch. They are the descendants of eighteenth-century Anabaptists who, as refugees from the Rhineland, settled in that part of America. They were therefore German or, in their mother tongue, *Deutsch*. The *Deutsch* was mistaken for Dutch! Dutchmen call themselves Netherlanders or Hollanders, a name not subject to any similar confusion of sound.

King Solomon's Stables

When in 1930 the famous ruins of Megiddo were excavated in the Holy Land, then still Palestine, the world was thrilled with the discovery of what was believed to be relics of 'King Solomon's stables'. There seemed to be no doubt as to the genuineness of the claim.

The unearthed stalls had room for almost 500 horses. They still contained revealing details, such as rows of pillars which had served simultaneously as supports for the roof and as hitching posts, with holes that had become polished by the countless times the horses' straps had been pulled through. Even the feeding troughs were still there. It was easy to imagine how the great king's horses had been kept and cared for in these stables. Did not the biblical 'Book of Kings' speak of this 'city of chariots', in which Solomon had provided 40,000 stalls for the horses drawing his carriages (I Kings 4:26)?

It was all an error. Further diggings — by Professor Y. Yadin in 1960 — showed beyond a shadow of a doubt that the so-called complex of 'King Solomon's stables' had been built long after the king's death in 931 B.C.! They belonged to King Ahab's time who, at the battle of Karkar in 835 B.C., rallied 2,000 chariots against the Assyrians.

The Zeppelin

Graf Zeppelin is not the real inventor of the dirigible airship called after him. The credit should go to Hungarian-born David Schwarz, who was the very first to construct such 'aircraft' (in 1892). A telegram from the German Government promising him greatly needed financial help (with the proviso of a successful testflight), excited him so much that he collapsed and died (in 1897). Subsequently, Graf Zeppelin (helped by Councillor Berg) purchased Schwarz's designs from his widow and, modifying them, built the airship which — with Schwarz forgotten — bears his name.

The Apostles' Creed

The 'Apostles' Creed', as a statement of faith and the epitome of the doctrines taught by the Apostles, used in the Western Church, originated at least three centuries after their death! Tersely worded, though possibly based on the Gospels (Matth. 28:19), none of its affirmations is Apostolic in words. Its title cannot be traced back beyond about A.D. 390, around which time the legend arose that the Creed was the joint composition of the twelve Apostles. Each of them had written one of its clauses. Its present-day text was first quoted in a manuscript going back only to the eighth century.

America

America is called after Amerigo Vespucci, a Florentine navigator who least deserved to be so honoured. A combination of circumstances by-passed Columbus whose name, if any man's, should thus have been perpetuated.

Vespucci was a somewhat enigmatic figure. He made himself widely known by accounts he published of voyages he had undertaken to the newly-discovered regions across the Atlantic and which he — cleverly — sent to people of renown and influence. Though his claim roused controversy and doubt on the part of experts, they gained wide currency among the general public. All that people seemed to remember of Columbus was that he had been mistaken in assuming that he had merely reached India.

In a pamphlet Vespucci published in 1503, entitled 'New World', he was the first to suggest that this should be the very name of the land across the Atlantic, 'There was no knowledge of it among our ancestors, and it is a totally new thing to all who hear of it.'

No wonder that he became ever more identified with the new territory. This prompted Martin Waldseemüller, a young German cartographer, on a global map he prepared for a work printed at St Dié in Lorraine, to 'label' the new continent Amerigo, Vespucci's Christian name. He justified his choice by the fallacious belief that 'since Amerigo Vespucci has discovered a fourth part of the world, I do not see any reason why anyone should rightfully object to calling this part after him'.

Latinized, Amerigo became Americus. However, as the other continents of the world were called after women, Vespucci's name underwent a change of sex as it were, and — in consonance with Africa and Asia — in its Latin feminine form, was rendered America.

Greenland and Iceland

Greenland is far from green. It is an island of ice and snow. Indeed, a great part of it is arctic wasteland, very much like Europe used to be during the Ice Age. In parts the thickness of the ice covering the land exceeds 1,500 metres. Only its coastal 'rim' (certainly in itself making up a vast area) is ice-free.

Eric the Red purposely chose its misleading name. Banished from Iceland for three years for killing two men in a feud, he arrived in (the future) Greenland. As a resourceful Viking navigator, he explored the island and decided to colonize it.

Like any good promoter and developer nowadays, he was convinced that if a place is given an attractive name, people will come to it. For this purpose he called (in about A.D. 985) the inhospitable island 'Green Land'. His plan worked and resulted in the arrival of twenty-five migrant ships. (From this icy Greenland Vikings sailed forth to discover North America, many centuries before Columbus set foot on American soil. They were led by Leif Ericsson, Eric's son.)

Iceland is not nearly as cold as its name suggests. It abounds in hot springs, volcanoes and geysers. The very name 'geyser' is Icelandic. Some 150 volcanoes have erupted on the island since the Ice Age, thirty of them since the country was settled. During the past 500 years one third of the world's lava spurted forth in Iceland. The enormous thermal activity of the country, duly harnessed, supplies the population with heat and constant hot water which is piped into people's homes. The natural heat is also utilized for greenhouses enabling them to grow flowers and fruit, including grapes and even bananas, all through the year. It is intriguing to know that during the Middle Ages it was believed that the very gateway to hell was situated in one of the volcanic craters of this country, notwithstanding the island's name which conjures up the bitter cold.

Cambridge

Cambridge, so famous a university city, shows by its very name how even a centre of learning can become a victim of mistakes.

Obviously, Cambridge refers to a settlement established at a site where a bridge spanned the river Cam. However, it is not the Cam on which Cambridge is situated but the Gronte (the Celtic for 'bog')! A stream recorded as early as A.D. 745, its name was corrupted into Granta. A bridge built across it, almost inevitably became known as Grantebricde. It was a name the Normans found difficult to pronounce. Accommodating it to their tongue, they changed it into Cantebridge. Eventually, further 'streamlined', this became Cambridge, resulting in the mistaken assumption that the city was on the Cam and not the Gronte which, to add insult to injury, is now one of the Cam's tributaries.

Eros in Piccadilly Circus

Anyone who has visited London knows the famous statue of Eros, the God of Love, standing at the very centre of Piccadilly Circus. Its description is a telling example of how love and sex may creep into the most unexpected places.

Eros' is a mistaken identity. The sculpture was designed by Sir Alfred Gilbert to top the memorial fountain he was commissioned to build in memory of the (seventh) Earl of Shaftesbury, the renowned Victorian philanthropist. Fittingly, the 'winged archer' portrays — not Eros — but 'the Angel of Christian Charity'.

The Red Square

The Red Square in Moscow was not so called because of the association of that colour with communism. In fact, the name pre-existed the Red revolution. To Russians red has always been a beautiful and attractive colour. To speak of a square as 'red' therefore was not meant to affirm a political conviction, but expressed aesthetic delight and splendour. No doubt, an additional factor in the choice of name was the similarity in sound of the Russian words for 'red' (*krasny*) and 'beauty' (*krasivy*).

Lead Pencil

Lead pencils never contained lead. But because in the sixteenth century people mistook as lead the thin stick of a compound of graphite and clay then used for writing, their error persisted, and the description was adopted worldwide. As it were, it became indelible in the human mind, and no evidence to the contrary was able to erase it. The mistake was possibly suggested by an old custom to draw lines on paper by means of a leaden plummet.

India Paper

India paper does not come from India. Its original homes were China and Japan! However, because the product was brought from the Far East to Europe in ships engaged in the India trade, it was identified with that country. In Britain India paper was pioneered by the original Oxford University Press, who first used it for the printing of Bibles and prayerbooks. It is rather odd that religion and learning — both sticklers for truth — thus combined in giving currency to a deceptive name.

India Ink

Like the paper, India ink has no Indian connection. It was first made by the Chinese. They produced it by combining lamp-black with gum, which they moulded into (at times slightly perfumed) sticks. Correctly, therefore, the ink should be referred to as Chinese, as the logical French actually did. As in the case of India paper, the misnomer goes back to people wrongly identifying the product with the ships importing it.

India Rubber

It is appropriate in a book on mistakes to mention a 'tool' to correct them. In this respect mankind owes an immense debt to the simple (India) rubber.

Mistakes breed other mistakes. The error that mistook America for India and hence regarded its native population as (Red) Indians, created the *India* rubber.

It goes back to Columbus' days and his second voyage to the New World that took him to Haiti. On landing on the island, the Spaniards were enthralled to see its inhabitants play with balls that bounced. These were made of a substance, completely unknown in Europe, which oozed out from incisions made in the bark of certain trees. Natives called it in their tongue 'weeping wood', a description which, rather disfigured — via the Spanish and French — reached England as *caoutchouc*. When in 1770 the English chemist Joseph Priestley accidentally discovered that this elastic substance was able to *rub out* pencil marks, he called it 'rubber', a name which has never been erased. In fact, not even its association with the mistaken India has been 'rubbed out'.

Hebrew Letters

Present-day so-called Hebrew letters, in reality are Syrian square script! This differs considerably from the original Hebrew still found on ancient inscriptions.

The Syrian script replaced the Hebrew around the fourth century B.C., when the Jews began to use it in Babylonia. From there it was introduced into Judea. The new alphabet was then officially adopted and all biblical writings in existence at the time were transcribed from the old alphabet into the new.

Arab Numerals

There is nothing Arab in Arab figures. They stem from India. Arab traders visiting the country, brought them to North Africa. Because it was from there that Arab Moors (in the tenth century) introduced them into Spain, they were thought to be Arabic. As so often in the naming of things, once again, not the originator but the importer is remembered.

Europeans did not take long to realize how superior the simple 'Arab' numerals were to the commonly used, rather complicated Roman 'figures', particularly so in calculations. Nevertheless, it took another six centuries before the 'Arab' ciphers completely superseded them.

Catgut

Cat lovers will be happy with this misnomer. There is nothing from inside the feline on string instruments. The so-called catgut comes from the intestines of sheep.

How the cat crept into this error has been variously explained.

'Kit' used to be the name for a small fiddle, especially favoured by dancing masters. It was easy to confuse that (little-known) 'kit' with the ubiquitous 'kitten' and to imagine that violin strings were its posthumous contribution.

Another derivation suggests that the error was due to fast speaking. Slurring the words, 'cattle gut' was contracted, resulting in a linguistic shape-change from cattle to cat.

People who listened to a learner practising the violin, not very kindly compared the sound to caterwauling. This made them think that only a cat's gut could produce such noise.

The Turkey

A Christmas dinner would be incomplete without a turkey, just as ever since the first American Thanksgiving Day in 1621, the fowl is part of its (culinary) celebration. Who then would imagine that the bird's very name is an alias, a counterfeit? No bird could be further removed from Turkey than the turkey, which became the victim of a multiplicity of mistakes.

The turkey is an American bird, first domesticated in Mexico. From there (in 1530) Spaniards brought it to Europe. When eventually it reached England, the British confused it with the guinea fowl, an earlier African arrival (from Guinea). This had been misnamed a turkey, because 'Turkish traders' had imported it. It was a real mix-up.

Whalebone

Whales are the largest animals alive, and yet, para-doxically, they feed on some of the smallest creatures. They do so for a valid reason. Their gullet is rather narrow and, to enable them to swallow the right type of food, nature has provided them with a special straining system: plates attached to the mammal's jaw which take the place of teeth. Similar to man's fingernails, this 'sieve' is of a horny substance. Certainly, it is not bone. Never-theless it has become known as whale*bone*.

Surprising is the variety of use man made of it from earliest days. In the treeless region of the Orkney Islands, it helped him to prop up his turf roofs. It provided Eskimos with runners for their sledges. The first modern umbrellas had whalebone skeletons, which, no doubt, added to their weight and initial unpopularity.

The Flying Squirrel

The flying squirrel is a rodent that does not fly. It glides by means of parachute membranes, which are extensions of skin connecting its fore and hindlegs. It can cover only short distances.

The Camelhair Brush

The soft camelhair brush painters use, is made from the long hair of a squirrel!

The Firefly

The firefly does not belong to any genus of fly but to the beetle family. Americans refer to it much more appropriately as a lightning bug. Its flashes are produced by light organs located on the abdomen. Apart from conveying sexual messages, they also serve as a warning to predators, reminding them of this luminous insect's bitter taste. Nonetheless, some frogs ignoring the signal, devour so many fireflies that they themselves start glowing.

The Crayfish

The crayfish is not a fish but a crustacean — a crab. Resembling a small lobster, its favourite habitat is beneath rocks in the water.

The Spinnaker

Any boat rigged with a spinnaker carries the Egyptian Sphinx, though mutilated. The fanciful name goes back to the first vessel using that type of sail (in the 1870s). It did so in a race in the Solent, the channel extending between the Isle of Wight and the mainland of southern England.

On the occasion, the sail was still unnamed. When other yachts watched the boat so rigged forging ahead, they realized the value of the novel sail and adopted it. They called it by the name of the very boat that carried it, the Sphinx. A name not easy to pronounce, it was distorted into Spinxer, eventually to become the spinnaker! It has been suggested that its choice might have been influenced by the spanker, once hoisted as a fairweather sail, yet ultimately used to take advantage of a tail wind.

6 Misnomers — You Don't Mean What You Say

To introduce or address someone by the wrong name certainly can be embarrassing. No one likes to be mistaken or to display ignorance. And yet, misnomers have become so much part of our daily life that we use them without even the slightest inkling that we don't mean what we say. Examples extend from the description of an ordinary item to well-known phrases we use on the occasion of a birthday, a wedding or when simply opening a door. The occurrence of the phenomenon is so diverse and so common that, once realized, it makes one wonder how it ever came into being and is still retained.

'Many Happy Returns'
To wish anyone 'many happy returns of the day' on the date of his or her birthday is a custom, which no one ever questions. Nevertheless, it makes no sense. Everyone has only *one* birthday. As the word explicitly states, it is the day of his or her birth. All subsequent occasions are its anniversaries. What the congratulations should really express is the wish of 'many happy returns of the *anniversary* of your birthday'.

Walking Down the Aisle
To 'walk down the aisle' as a bride is still many a girl's wish. No bride ever does; she walks down the central nave!

Aisle — from the Latin *ala* for 'wing' — refers to the sides of a building. Its use for the passageway leading in between the pews is a misnomer.

When 'First Married'

Recalling the early days of their union, couples are wont to say, 'when we were first married'. Put this way, it might imply a previous marriage. Accurately, they ought to say, 'soon after we were married'.

A mere change of position, however, would avoid the confusion, without any substitution of words. 'First', instead of following the verb, should precede it. 'When first we were married' would exclude any misunderstanding or suggestion of a previous marriage.

To Answer The Door

Whenever we 'answer the door', we do not know what we are talking about. It is not the door that is answered, but the caller who knocks or rings the bell.

To Learn by Heart

It took man a long time to understand the specific function of the various organs of his body. Pride of place must go to the heart, and for an obvious reason. It made its presence felt, particularly so on occasions of excitement. Early on, its palpitations were (mis)taken as the cause (and not the effect) of happiness or distress. The heart came to be regarded as the very organ in which human feelings were produced. 'With all my heart' became an affirmation of sincerity, sympathy and devotion. At one time the heart was imagined to be the seat of the mind as well. This led to the belief that man thought and remembered with the heart, and not the brain.

It was unfortunate that Aristotle, the renowned Greek philosopher, made this mistake. As anything he wrote was accepted as absolute truth, countless generations after him copied his error. Actually, the fallacy of the view was discovered soon after Aristotle's death by the Greek surgeon and anatomist Herophilus. Founder of the School of Anatomy at Alexandria, he was among the first to conduct post-mortems and to examine and describe the brain. In spite of it, in the way of speaking, Aristotle has never been corrected so that we still 'remember' his mistakes and continue, senselessly, to describe memorizing as 'learning by heart'.

'You Can't Have Your Cake and Eat it Too'

That 'you can't have your cake and eat it too', at first seems a plausible reflection on life. You either spend your money or save it. You can't have it both ways.

The sequence of the phrase is illogical and reverses the order. Of necessity, you must first have your cake in order to be able to eat it. Hence, properly put, it should say, 'you cannot eat your cake and (still) have it'.

The Secretary

A secretary was so called because she was expected to keep secrets! (Of course, this applies also to male secretaries.) This was the original purpose of her employment. The name described her position of trust, now no longer recognized.

One mistake led to another, and the misconceived title gave birth to the modern 'confidential secretary', an unnecessary duplication of words. If only we knew what we say.

Rice Paper

Even rice has firmly engrained itself in the vocabulary of misnomers. The so-called rice paper Chinese and Japanese use for their beautiful scrollwork and opaque window panes, has no connection with rice. It contains nothing of the plant or its seeds.

Its 'rice' is made from the pith of a small Taiwanese tree-plant, belonging to the ivy or Ginseng family. After having been cut, its pith is pressed into sheets which constitute the 'paper'.

The Continents of Europe and Asia

To count Europe and Asia as separate 'continents' is a mistake. The Latin-derived term was coined to describe a continuous mass (of land) which is 'held together' (*contenere*) and not divided by an ocean. As Europe and Asia are joined over a distance of thousands of kilometres, they are *not* individual continents. Correctly, both should carry one name, as suggested by the rarely used Eurasia.

The Blue Danube

Johann Strauss' waltz the 'Blue Danube' has never lost its charm. It has outlived many other, once-popular tunes. Unfortunately, however, it has also been responsible for a misconception which, when discovered, is very disappointing. There is no beautiful 'blue' Danube. Far from being blue, the river is muddy!

The Red Sea

Commentators have taken pains to explain the colour of the Red Sea. Ever since the (third century B.C.) Greek translations of the Hebrew Bible (the *Septuagint*), its redness has been linked with the death of the Egyptians who, in their pursuit of the escaping Israelites were drowned in its waters. Oddly enough, no one considered the absurdity of the claim as, of course, drowned people do not bleed.

Other explanations suggested that the red colour was due to as diverse factors as the growth of corals, the reflection of either sunlight or of red sand or soil which either surrounded the waters or formed the sea-bed.

A simple reference to the original Hebrew text of the passage would have avoided the many false trails. This clearly states that the Egyptians drowned in the Sea of Reeds (*yam suf*). It did not take much effort or time, particularly in connection with the death of so many Egyptians, popularly to adopt the false notion which changed the 'reed' into 'red' and it has been the Red Sea ever since.

The Black Sea

In classical Greek times, Iranians populated the area surrounding the large body of water now known as the Black Sea. They could not fail but notice that its colour was considerably darker than that of the inland rivers. This made them refer to the sea as 'dark' — *axsaena*. Other people, unaware of the reason for the description, further 'blackened' the sea and that is how, in many tongues, it became wrongly known as the Black Sea.

This was not the only misnomer. It seemed as if that vast expanse of water attracted mistakes. To Greek ears, the Iranian *axsaena* sounded very much like their own word *axeinos* — 'inhospitable'.

This is understandable, as the entire region was renowned and feared for its violent storms, impenetrable fogs and thick cloud cover that obscured the sun. The prevailing atmosphere was one of oppressive darkness — dismal, foreboding and forbidding.

The similarity of sound made the Greeks shun the name altogether. To them it spelled evil — and if voiced, might even evoke it. Instead, they used a euphemism, calling the 'inhospitable sea' — *Pontos Aximos,* the 'friendly sea' — *Pontos Euximos.* In doing so, they hoped to placate and flatter the evil forces and buy their good will.

The 'friendly sea' has long been forgotten. The equally erroneous 'black sea', however, survives, misguiding those who take its name literally.

The Pacific Ocean

There is nothing particularly peaceful about the Pacific Ocean, a name it certainly does not merit. It has been the scene of many ferocious naval battles. Storms and hurricanes ravaging its waters, have wrecked many a ship and drowned countless sailors.

When (in 1520–22) Ferdinand Magellan, the Portuguese explorer, undertook his history-making first circumnavigation of the world, he did so from east to west. After passing through the wild and stormy waters that divided the southernmost tip of the Latin American mainland from Tierra del Fuego, he entered a sea that — in comparison — seemed calm and serene. The contrast was so great that he called it the 'peaceful ocean' — 'the Pacific' — from the Latin *pacificus*. It was a pacific ocean only relatively speaking.

Flying Fish
Fish never fly. They glide. The misnomer is due to inaccurate observation. They propel themselves at such accelerated speed that they are able to leap out of the water. Their extended fins then help them, not to fly, but to keep aloft, skimming the surface for considerable distances.

Magnetic Island
Magnetic Island, in Northern Queensland, is renowned for its beauty. When James Cook discovered it (in 1770), he erroneously imagined that it affected the compass of his ship. Believing that this was due to magnetic ore buried in its hills, he called it Magnetic Island. His assumption was proved wrong, but the name has never been changed.

Dentures
Vanity has often led man astray. Dentures — from the French *dent* — merely refer to (a set of) 'teeth'. However, those in need of false teeth, not wanting to draw undue attention to the loss of their own, call the replacement dentures. The misleading term has become so much accepted that, though the owner of artificial teeth may remove them every night, his denture is firmly stuck in man's dictionary, if not in his mouth.

Eyeteeth
Eyeteeth have nothing to do with the eyes, nor does their extraction have an effect on vision.

A much more appropriate name would be their

alternate, canine teeth. They help dogs and other carnivorous animals to tear the flesh from their prey.

The reason for the misnomer is not far to seek. The teeth are situated under the eyes, with their roots extending towards them. In fact, both eyes and teeth are served by a common network of nerves, which explains why at times a 'referred' toothache may be felt in the eye.

Eye Fatigue

What is ordinarily described as eye fatigue is not fatigue of the eye(ball) at all, but of its muscles. These may have been used too much by such diverse factors as insufficient illumination of the object looked at or a bad position in which the 'viewer' or reader is placed.

Arteries

Arteries are the vessels which convey the blood from the heart to the various parts of the body. But their very name — literally — empties them out and, strange to believe, suggests that they contain nothing but 'air' (*aer* in Greek).

The reason for this error and misnomer shows how misleading partial observation can be. Early anatomists dissecting the dead found that, whilst the veins contained blood, the arteries seemed 'empty'. Puzzled, they came to believe that the arteries were airducts which served the vital 'spirit' dwelling in man. In this context, it is interesting to note that Hippocrates very appropriately called the windpipe an *arteria*.

Having Blood Pressure

Man has been victim of many diseases. He has equally suffered from misconceptions as to their causes and cures and the right way to preserve his good health. Someone who says that he has 'blood pressure', really confirms that he is alive. No one could live without it. What he wants to convey is that his blood pressure is elevated. There is no fixed 'normal' blood pressure either. It varies according to circumstances and many individual factors.

Heartburn

Heartburn is not connected with the heart. The burning sensation in the chest comes from the stomach. When suffering from a bout of indigestion, acid is regurgitated into the oesophagus, which is located behind the heart.

'I've Got a Temperature'

'I've got a temperature', is a common complaint of patients with fever. They really do not mean what they say. Everyone must have some temperature, whether measured in Celsius or Fahrenheit.

What the sick person actually wants to express is that his or her temperature is raised above the normal. This, indeed, is a — sick — misnomer.

The Ten-Gallon Hat

Almost proverbial is the ten-gallon hat worn by Americans in the 'Old West', particularly so in Texas. Its description is taken to refer to its enormous size, which would conform with all the other Texan superlatives. The implication, of course, is that the hat was so large that it could be filled with ten gallons of liquid. This is an error due to a linguistic 'mix-up'. In this case the gallon is not the unit of capacity, but the Spanish *galon* for 'braid'.

The hat is not Texan at all but stems from Mexico. When Spaniards occupied the country, they wore sombreros because the wide brims protected their faces from the burning sun. Spaniards' love of beauty made them embellish this utilitarian brim with braid. The more of it they used the happier they were. Some men thus wore a hat with ten different braids. Very accurately and without exaggeration, it was a ten *galon* hat.

When the Americans adopted the Spanish head-covering, they acquired its Spanish name as well. Continuing to call it a ten gal(l)on hat, the Spanish (*galon*) braid was soon misunderstood and mistaken for the liquid measure. This created the ten-gallon hat.

The Tartan

A painting displays the artist's signature in one of its corners. Many a garment has woven into the (linguistic) texture of its name its place of origin. At times, this might be so well camouflaged that it is almost beyond recognition. Calico comes from Calicut in India, worsted from Worstead in Norfolk, England. Denim originated in (the southern French town of) Nîmes and recalling its source was named *de Nîmes* — 'from Nîmes'.

The Scotch tartan covers more territory — at least speechwise. Certainly, it has no connection with the Tartars, as some might imagine. It is a mistake, however, to think that the tartan was the original Scottish Highland attire. When the Gaels first arrived in Scotland from Ireland, they wore a distinctive kind of shirt, known as *léine* in Gaelic. Mostly made of linen, it had a yellowish tint. This led the English to describe it as a saffron shirt. Early on, it was marked with stripes to indicate the rank of the wearer. Seven stripes, of which one was purple, distinguished the High King, whilst, indicative of the appreciation of scholarship among the Scots already in early days, the Ollamh, the Chief Man of Learning, could be recognized by his six stripes!

Equally erroneous is the assumption that when the tartan became part of the Highlanders' vocabulary and dress, the word designated its design, the chequered pattern with its specific colours. Coming from the French *tartaine*, 'tartan' referred to a certain fabric — a mixture of wool and linen. The French themselves had borrowed the term from the Spaniards, who called a silken material *tiritaña*, most likely because of the swishing sound it made, as the root of the word was the Spanish for 'rustle'.

There is another mistaken view attached to the tartans. This is that, from the beginning, their various types were the deliberate historical choice of the individual clans, so that they could be identified. However, this was not so. It was by mere chance, the local availability of dye-stuffs, that made a clan wear certain colours. Many of the so-called clan-tartans of today, in fact, are of recent origin, not going back much beyond the beginning of the nineteenth century!

Moth-Eaten

Moths do not feed on clothes. It is therefore a mistake to describe the damaged material as 'moth-eaten'. The imputation is based on fallacious circumstantial evidence. Discovering clothes ruined after moths have been seen flying out of the closet, these are wrongly blamed as the culprits.

What actually happens is that moths lay their eggs on material they favour and the developing larvae eat the cloth. Once these have become moths, the harm has already been done. The holes are the result of their prenatal activity.

Chamois Leather

There is nothing of the chamois, that goat-like alpine animal, in chamois leather. It is made from the underside of sheepskin.

Air Pockets

It is wrong to assume that all misnomers are carry-overs from non-scientific days. We have our share in creating them.

One such common error concerns the so-called 'air pockets' blamed for a plane's being tossed about. They do not exist. The unpleasant experience is due to a totally different circumstance. It occurs when a plane, mostly whilst flying through a cloud (particularly of the cumulus type) is caught by a very strong up or down current. This and not an air pocket or vacuum causes the — very uncomfortable — sudden drop or lift.

Oxygen

Oxygen is an essential for life. Its very name, coined (in 1779) by the French chemist Lavoisier, perpetuates a misconception on his part. He erroneously believed that this gaseous element was vital in the formation of acids. He therefore called it by a name which specifically referred to this imagined faculty of 'giving rise to acids', oxygen — from *oxus,* the Greek for 'sharp'. His mistake has never been rectified.

The Crescent Moon

'Crescent', from the Latin *crescere,* means 'growing'. That is why in music when the volume of tone increases we speak of a crescendo. However, we thoughtlessly describe the lunar sickle in the night sky as a crescent moon, irrespective of whether it is in its increasing or decreasing phase, the first or the last quarter. Correctly, the term should be applied exclusively to the waxing moon.

Mohammedanism

Mohammedanism is a misnomer and offensive to those following Mohammed's faith. Just as Christianity expresses the worship of Christ, so the name could imply the apotheosis of Mohammed, totally foreign to his followers. To deify him would be contrary to Moslem belief.

Moslems regard Mohammed as a prophet, in fact, as the greatest of all — the 'seal of prophecy'. Succeeding Abraham, Moses and Christ, he is said to have surpassed them and no other prophet will follow him. However, he was still only a man.

The correct name of the faith is Islam. An Arab term and concept, it speaks of the faithfuls' complete 'submission' to the will of God. Accordingly, its adherents should not be called Mohammedans, but Moslems — derived from Islam.

The Anecdote

In Greek *an* is a prefix meaning 'not'. It indicates a lack. Anyone who is *an*onymous is 'without' a name, he is 'not' known. *An*aemia describes a deficiency of red blood cells. Few would suspect such negative message in an *an*ecdote.

Anecdotes are considered entertaining accounts of incidents from someone's life. They make most popular reading. However, their description as an anecdote implies the exact opposite. Taken literally, they should be a closely guarded secret and told, if at all, only in strictest confidence. The term combined the Greek negative *an* with *ekdotos*, 'published'. It is something unpublished, a secret history.

This, in fact, is the very sense in which *Anecdotes* were first used in literature, as the title of a collection of stories attributed to Procopius, sixth-century Byzantine historian and prefect of Constantinople. He had chosen it for a very good reason. The anecdotes were scandalous accounts from the lives of his most prominent contemporaries, many of whom filled the highest offices. Their public circulation would have had serious consequences. Hence, he 'published' them 'privately', as a hidden supplement, so to speak, to his official and renowned *Histories*. The name he gave them was therefore well chosen and appropriate, meaning what it said.

The Divan

A divan may now serve as a comfortable couch in a home. Those reclining on it do not realize how, far from being a piece of furniture, the divan once fulfilled an entirely different purpose and was reserved for the highly educated. In Persian and Arabic cultures, 'divan' described a collection of poems written on individual leaves which were bound together.

The deterioration of such intellectual delight into a backless sofa is hard to understand. It happened gradually. To begin with, people thought that such a 'brochure' could equally serve to register accounts, and it became a kind of ledger. Subsequently, its name was transferred to the office in which the ledger was 'kept'. In Turkey, this was the Council Chamber, where the judicial body met, to record their code of law. Finally, the Council members became known by the name of their meeting place as the divan.

European visitors were intrigued by the cushioned bench on which the councillors and judges took their seat and which ran along the chamber's walls. Mixing up names, they wrongly assumed that this was a divan! That is how the original 'collection of poetry' — a volume of leaves — became a mere sofa. Introduced into Europe as a fashionable and, at times, most elaborate adaptation of Oriental comfort, people were unaware of the confusion it wrought.

A Loaf of Bread

Bread once was the 'staff of life' and to 'break' it a solemn occasion. That we still speak of 'breaking bread' goes back to Old Testament times, when the unleavened bread eaten by the ancient Hebrews, because of its thinness and texture, could not be cut but had to be broken. Jesus did so at the Last Supper. The introduction of cutlery was a much later refinement, at the time frowned upon by people who much preferred to use the dexterous fingers God had given them.

To speak of a 'loaf of bread' is a contradiction in terms. The original 'bread' was merely a portion, a fragment, literally a 'crumb'. A left-over from the meal, the morsel was offered to hungry beggars calling at the door. 'Broken bits of a loaf' continued to be the meaning of any bread till the thirteenth century. To speak of 'bread-crumbs' therefore is to say the same thing twice over!

Loaf, an Old English term, denotes anything that was expected to 'rise'. A loaf of bread thus linked crumbs with the gaining of height, rather an odd phenomenon and, certainly, an indigestible combination of words in the realm of language.

Porridge

Originally, porridge was a 'leek broth'. Its name consists of a strange sort of mixture. It joins part of the (Latin for) 'leek' — *porrum* — with a portion of the biblical mess of 'pottage' for which Esau erroneously is believed to have sold his birthright to Jacob and which is a corruption of the French 'soup', *potage*. The Scots then put oatmeal into the porridge where, in spite of what its name says, it has remained ever since.

Arrowroot
The arrow in arrowroot is deceptive. It has nothing to do with the pointed weapon. Nevertheless, it has been assumed to be so real that most convincing explanations have been given for its presence in the name of this starch-yielding plant. This was so called, people believed, because Red Indians had discovered the healing property of the sap of its tuber in the treatment of wounds inflicted by poisoned arrows. The sap was supposed to absorb the venom.

The arrow in (the name of) the plant is derived from the American Indian word *aru-aru* for 'flour' or 'meal of meals'. There was good reason for this. The starch obtained from its roots proved most nutritious and easy to digest, so much so that gruel made from it was given to children and invalids.

The Red Herring
A reference to 'a red herring' may mean one of two completely different things. Metaphorically, it might be used to denounce an evasive action or remark intended to divert people's attention from the real issue. In this sense, it recalls the practice of fox hunters whilst training their dogs to drag a smoked 'red herring' across the animal's trail; its strong smell was intended to cover up the quarry's scent.

The real red herring is not red at all. Even when dried, smoked and salted, it retains its original colour. However, because the treatment turned its eyes red, the entire fish has been wrongly tainted as being red altogether.

Peanuts and Monkeynuts

Anything considered of trifling importance or little value is often described as 'peanuts'. It is a most ill-chosen comparison. Tests made by the University of Georgia, USA, to ascertain the nutritional significance of the peanut, proved its tremendous food value. Half a kilo of peanut butter was equal to 1⅛ kilo of steak, four litres of milk or thirty-two eggs.

George Washington Carver, son of slave parents, devoted most of his life to the research of the peanut. He was able to show its extraordinary usefulness: how it could serve as the source of more than 300 different products! His discovery was historical, as it revolutionized the entire American south. A unique museum, dedicated to Carver and the peanut, is now part of the 'black' Tuskegee University, in Alabama.

There is yet another fallacy about the peanut. It is misnamed. The peanut, colloquially also known as monkey or groundnut, is not a nut. It belongs to the legume family and is a pea! Much more correct therefore is its African description as goober pea.

Coffee Beans

Coffee beans are not beans but seeds. The misnomer was the result of their beanlike shape.

Chocolate

No one realizes the true meaning of chocolate. In spite of its sweetness, its name — from the Aztec *xococ* and *atl* — means 'bitter water'. It was a drink brewed and popularized by the Mayas and Aztecs who in its preparation mixed crushed cocoa beans and ground maize-corn, with a little water. They then flavoured the 'potion' with honey, fragrant herbs and chili. It was the latter that gave the drink its bitter taste, so completely different from that of our present-day chocolate, and responsible for its now so inappropriate name.

Honeysuckle
The name of honeysuckle suggests that bees extract honey from it. This is a fallacy. In actual fact, the honeysuckle is of no value to bees.

Ammunition
Fusion has played an unexpected role in the creation of modern ammunition. It has changed its total meaning. However, it did so not in the realm of explosives but in the world of mistakes.

Originally, a city's 'fortification' was known by the French *la munition*. Derived from the Latin *munitio,* the description referred to the 'building' of a defensive wall. Those not acquainted with French, mistook and misspelled the word. They detached the 'a' from (the French article) *la,* to link it with the (French) 'wall', thereby transforming *la munition* into *l'ammunition.* This produced (in English) the world's first 'ammunition'. At the beginning, it continued to denote a mere rampart, only subsequently to take on its explosive connotation.

Pistols
Pistols are called after Pistoria, the Italian city in Tuscany situated north-west of Florence and famous for a great variety of wares manufactured there, including arms. The pistol, one of its products, was not a handgun at all but a sharp-bladed dagger!

7 They Really Took It Seriously

Astounding is the number of misconceptions that have haunted man. Some are so fantastic that we can hardly believe that anyone could have taken them seriously. Nevertheless, for hundreds of years, the most bizarre fallacies dominated people's thoughts, determined their attitudes and controlled their practices. They reflect the extent of human folly and teach us to be wary of what seems to us so perfectly correct and unquestionable.

Gout — a Rich Man's Disease
To suffer from gout was once almost a distinction. Those indulging in rich food and plenty of drink were thought to be specially prone to the complaint which hence was confined to the upper class and the rich. Though this may have helped psychologically those having the affliction in raising their 'status', the notion does not conform with facts.

White Spots on Fingernails
The appearance of small white spots on fingernails has intrigued, worried and pleased people, all depending on what they 'recognized' in it. Some saw in the spots irrefutable evidence of an untruthful character, each spot representing a lie! Others, more fortunately, were of the firm belief that they were 'good luck spots', ensuring a happy life.

The spots have no occult or ethical bearing. Mostly a physiological blemish, they result from dead cells near the root of the nail being pushed forward, to become visible as 'white spots'.

Birthmarks

Mystified by birthmarks, people have rightly wondered what caused them. Some genuinely believed that they were the result of a fright experienced by the mother whilst pregnant. They even imagined to recognize in the mark the very object that had been responsible for the emotional upset.

The notion created the custom for pregnant women to gaze at beautiful paintings and listen to good music. They were convinced that in so doing, they would be spared excitement and their child be endowed with artistic gifts.

Shocks do not cause birthmarks nor do they leave any physical traces on the foetus. It has rightly been pointed out that, if it were so, many a baby would look like a speckled hen. Generally, a birthmark is a malformation of a blood vessel.

Eye Mistakes

Eyesight is one of man's most precious gifts, and blindness is a terrible affliction. This has made him pay close attention to anything related to his eyes, resulting in many observations that were correct and helpful but also in numerous illusions, fallacies and abstruse notions.

The visual organ was seen as a give-away revealing a person's character or certain psychological dispositions. Anyone therefore who averted his eyes, stared or peeped gave away something of himself. It was part of his body language.

Preoccupation with the eye extended from the imagined possession of an 'evil eye' to the voyeur who has become a sex-obsessed 'seer'. Man is so concerned with the eye, it is no wonder he has searched everywhere for some means to protect and increase his vision. He was equally anxious to shield himself from being 'overlooked' which, in occult language, meant to be exposed to the evil eye of another person. So prominent in life, it is no wonder that the eye has become part of the alphabet, in which its picture created the letter 'o'. The eye has been responsible as well for countless expressions in everyday vocabulary, from the short-sighted to the far-sighted, from people who have clear views to those who are jaundiced or are possessed by the green-eyed monster.

Ill Effects of a Jaundiced Eye

Because jaundice made the whites of people's eyes (and their skin) turn yellow, it was believed that those suffering from the sickness saw everything tinged in that colour. Their entire outlook on life was changed, becoming morose and bitter. Though this view has long been discarded as erroneous and unscientific, we continue to describe such a state of mind as 'jaundiced'! (The word jaundice is derived from Old French for 'yellow'.)

Vision and Bedrest

One of the earliest English books on the eye was written by Dr Walter Bayley, court physician of Queen Elizabeth I. In it he expressed the view (held for centuries after him) that a person's position in bed while asleep affected his daytime vision. It was desirable to go to sleep on the left side, later on to turn over to the right. Exposure of the eyes to the rays of the moon whilst in bed, was inadvisable, as it would harm the eye. For many years thus, people paid special attention to the manner in which they rested.

Reading in Bed

Deeply-rooted was the general (fallacious) belief that reading in bed was injurious to the eyes. (However, it is wise to have good light and to be so positioned that any muscular strain, particularly in the neck and shoulders, is avoided.)

Needlework
Incorrectly it was thought that fine needlework would ruin the eyesight. All it can do is to tire the eyes.

A Mirror of Sickness
A long-held, weird fallacy claimed that the condition of health of every part of the body could be recognized in the eyes. Diagrams and charts published for such 'iris diagnosis', allocated specific sections of the eye to each individual organ. These were imagined to reflect whether the organ functioned well or was diseased. Studying, for instance, a spot at '3 o'clock' in the iris was thought to reveal the state of the oesophagus, whilst the sector situated at '5 o'clock' was believed to disclose the health or malfunction of the bladder. In actual fact, only certain facets of bodily health show up in the eye. Typical examples concern the hardening of the arteries, elevated blood pressure, a high cholesterol level, diabetes, and the existence of a brain tumour. Each of these abnormalities have specific indications, typical of them.

Stye in the Eye
People were convinced that a stye on the eyelid could be cured by the touch of a golden wedding ring. Mere folklore, this is based on the ancient myth that gold, as a precious royal metal, was endowed with miraculous curative power.

Looks Can Kill
We still speak of people 'looking daggers' at us, using the expression as a figure of speech. We do not realize that it perpetuates yet another once strongly-held view that in certain individuals hatred could generate demonic power of such force that their withering glance was able to inflict untold harm, if not death.

Murderer's Image on Pupil
People seriously believed that a murdered person's eyes

retained the image of the killer. When Rudyard Kipling in his story 'At the End of the Passage' adopted this false notion, he further popularized it. In 1908, people were still so convinced of the validity of this myth that at a famous murder trial they demanded the examination of the victim's eyes, as this would, undoubtedly, reveal the murderer's identity.

No retina can retain a picture. Though the eye works like a camera, to 'hold' the picture as in photography, a chemical fixer would be needed which no eye provides.

Black Eye and Raw Meat

The traditional treatment of a black eye was to apply raw meat. It was thought to be an effective remedy. It is of no particular help. All it might do is to reduce the swelling, equally achieved by anything else that is cool and moist.

Skylarking

Before it was realized that scurvy was a disorder due to Vitamin C deficiency, on their long voyages sailors became its frequent victims. Unaware of the real cause, they applied many a useless remedy. Additional exercise was thought to combat the disease. Therefore it became the daily routine of seamen and, in fact, part of their duty, every evening to dance the hornpipe, then popular in the British Isles and so called because it was performed to the accompaniment of that instrument. The customary tune played was the 'Song of the Skylark'. To let off steam, the sailors soon changed the nightly practice into an occasion of fun and merriment.

This gave 'skylarking' the sense of fooling about and playing pranks. Even when the true cause of scurvy had been discovered and, to prevent it, British sailors were given limes (responsible for their nickname 'limeys') they continued their 'skylarking'.

A 'flighty' term, it soon reached land and has remained a telling description ever since, in spite of having been conceived in error.

Feed a Cold and Starve a Fever

The proverbial advice to 'feed a cold and starve a fever' has misguided many a credulous patient. He genuinely imagined that it was logical to eat plenty of food when suffering from a cold, as this would strengthen his power of resistance, enabling him to shake off the infection quickly. The opposite 'treatment' in the case of a fever was sure to reduce it.

Neither counsel is medically sound. Overeating is never beneficial, particularly so when in bed. On the other hand, a fever dehydrates the body which therefore requires lots of fluid.

Though at first sight the adage seems clear and simple, it is deceptive in its ambiguity. It has been questioned whether it exhorted a patient 'to feed a cold and to starve a fever' or, rightly understood, warned him that if he ate too much while having a cold, he would subsequently run a temperature which then he had to starve!

Cobwebs Stop Bleeding

Cobwebs must have intrigued man early on. It seemed that some supernatural power gave the intricate texture woven by a spider the ability to trap insects of considerable size and stop them from escaping. The belief in the occult gift of the web made people attribute a magical medicinal property to the cobweb, that of stopping wounds from bleeding.

Shakespeare not only accepted this fallacy, but further spread it when, in *A Midsummer Night's Dream* (Act III, scene 1), he made Bottom say, 'I shall desire you of more acquaintance, good Master Cobweb: if I cut my finger, I shall make bold with you.'

Cobwebs do not stop bleeding but can create additional trouble. Often spun in dark corners, they catch dirty flies and harbour microbes. Applied to wounds, instead of stopping the bleeding, they thus might easily infect them.

Nose Bleeding

Fanciful, indeed, are the various procedures people followed to stop nose bleeding. They placed a key or an icebag at the back of the neck, or tilted the head back.

None of these treatments is of any use. In the majority of cases, the bleeding will stop by itself. The apparent success of the home cures merely coincides with the natural cessation of nose bleeding. When tilting the head, the flow of blood is only redirected down the throat, which, instead of improving the situation, might create complications, such as vomiting and nausea.

To Count Sheep

Those suffering from insomnia are often told to count sheep. It can do no harm. It costs nothing and will have no unpleasant side-effects.

The sleep-inducing effect of the 'count-down' is not the result of the sheep, but of autosuggestion. One may as well count cats and dogs, or well-nigh anything so long as it empties the mind of other thoughts which keep one awake. Certainly, the steady and repetitive counting is soporific. The best advice to insomniacs is to make themselves so tired that they will not have even the inclination or time to count anything before dropping off.

The Healing 'Royal Touch'

When royalty was still looked upon as divine, kings were believed to be endowed with exclusive curative powers. Their 'royal touch' was imagined to cure diseases which were beyond the ordinary doctor's ken. This applied particularly to scrofula, dubbed 'the king's evil'.

Those thus royally 'treated' were given specially stamped gold coins. (Records show that their presentation cost the Royal Exchequer an annual amount of £3,000, a vast sum at the time.) It was a peculiar form of medication supplied by the king. His patients treasured the 'touch stones', by which name the gold coins became known, often wearing them as an amulet.

Shakespeare recalls the royal 'practice' in *Macbeth*, in which Malcolm refers to it as 'most miraculous work ... I've seen [the king] do': how he cured 'strangely-visited people. All swoll'n and ulcerous, pitiful to the eye. The mere despair of surgery ... hanging a gold stamp about their necks, put on with holy prayers.'

The administering of the 'royal touch' can be traced back in England to King Edward the Confessor (d. 1066). (In France it was known even earlier.) Dr Samuel Johnson was 'touched' by Queen Anne in 1745.

The 'royal touch' was imagined to be so potent that its magical power was thought to be transferrable to objects in the king's possession. The mere touching of anything he had touched would provide the cure! A typical example relates to a certain Mrs Brathwayt who had suffered from 'the king's evil'. She had been cured by touching a torn and dirty handkerchief, used by young King Charles after the battle of Worcester, when suffering from bouts of nose-bleeding.

Scrofula was a glandular disease, now diagnosed as a tubercular infection of the lymph glands. Its symptoms were a lumpy swelling along the sides of the neck and above the collarbone. The name is derived from the Middle English for a 'breeding sow' (*scrofa*), presumed to be most vulnerable to the sickness. Its popular description as 'the king's evil' has an unfortunate ambiguity, subject to misunderstanding. It did not infer, as its name might suggest, that the disease was caused by the king who, therefore, alone could take it away again. All it wanted to emphasize was that only royalty — by its mysterious divine power — had the ability (and, later on, the prerogative) to cure the affliction.

Warts and Toads

Man was repulsed by the ugliness of a toad. Fairy tales around the world told of many a human who, in punishment for a misdeed, was changed into the hideous creature. The toad was shunned as well — not in the realm of fantasy but in everyday life — because people were convinced that by touching it, they would grow warts. The reason was the wartlike appearance of the toad's skin. This was thought, by mere touch or by sympathetic magic, to infect those handling it, resulting in the growth of ugly 'blotches' of a similar kind.

Night Air and Malaria

Malaria was believed to be caused by 'bad (night) air'. People imagined that the disease struck those who lived near swampy ground, from which poisonous fumes rose, especially at night. That is why they called the sickness *mal aria,* from the Italian for 'bad air'. It made them close their windows tightly at night and wonder why, in spite of their precaution, they caught the infection! Once again, it was Shakespeare who popularized the fallacy through one of his plays, *The Tempest.* When, eventually, it was discovered that it was not bad air but the bite of the anopheles mosquito which was responsible for the sickness, its misleading description as 'malaria' was still not abandoned.

Menstruation

A woman's monthly period has mystified and frightened man. In primitive cultures this resulted in numerous taboos. Adding to her physical discomfort, she was shunned, if not chased away. 'Civilized' man continued to hold many a misconception and to observe, with great caution and care, meaningless practices associated with this monthly 'visitation'.

Menstruation and the Phases of the Moon

The mere coincidence of the menstrual cycle (of twenty-eight days) with the duration of a lunar month (of approximately 29½ days), led to the wrong conclusion that a woman's 'period', like the ebb and flow of the sea, was controlled by the lunar phases!

Coitus During Menstruation

Coitus during menstruation was thought to be ill-advised, in fact, dangerous. It was imagined to affect the physical and mental health of future children, who would be born weak and insane. Even the man having intercourse with her could jeopardize his health. He might contract measles or syphilis!

Menstruation and Water

An inherent awe of blood created other (unfounded) avoidances. The menstruating woman refrained from swimming or taking a bath. She was convinced that her period made her uterus open up to suck the water into her body. The heat of the bathwater, furthermore, would increase her blood-flow so much that it might induce anaemia. On the other hand, cold water would chill her body and with it her power of resistance which, already greatly lowered, would make her an easy victim of disease.

Masturbation Harmful

Great anguish has been caused by the long-held belief that masturbation harmed both body and mind. Female frigidity, male impotence, and insanity have been quoted as possible (frightening) effects of the practice, decried as 'self-abuse'!

The fallacy goes back to the misinterpretation of a biblical account. This tells of Onan, the brother-in-law of a childless widow who, according to Hebrew legislation, was obliged to marry her to ensure the perpetuation of his deceased brother's name. Unwilling to do so, though joining her in the bedroom, he 'spilled his semen on to the ground' (Gen. 38:1-11). In punishment for disobeying the law, the Bible tells, he was put to death. His action (or rather, neglect of action) was later misunderstood. It was believed that it was not his refusal to marry his sister-in-law but his masturbation that had led to his death. This explains why masturbation is also known as Onanism and is considered a sin. With the added imagined physical and psychological threats, masturbation came to haunt man and, instead of relieving his tension, greatly increased it.

Virgins and Cure of Venereal Disease
Medieval folk-medicine had the absurd notion that men suffering from venereal disease could be cured by having intercourse with a virgin. She herself, it was further assumed, would not be infected whilst playing her healing role.

Lunacy
Madness has been explained by the craziest ideas. Those thus afflicted were thought to be 'possessed' by God which made men take their words as a divine message. On the other hand, it was surmised that people became insane because an evil spirit had entered their body. To heal them, it was necessary to exorcise the demon.

Most of all, however, it was seriously maintained that exposure to the moon resulted in madness. Therefore, it was described as 'lunacy' (from the Latin *luna* for 'moon'). Excessive masturbation, over-indulgence in sex and even bad teeth were cited as other causes of an unbalanced mind.

Man One Rib Less Than Woman
Because the Bible tells that God had created Eve out of one of Adam's ribs, people actually believed that every man had one rib less than a woman. Anatomy is a comparatively modern science and, for thousands of years, the dissecting of a corpse was condemned as blasphemous. Therefore no one ever dared to check up on the accuracy of the claim.

Ever since Adam's loss, so a story goes, every man travels far and wide to find his missing rib. Some never succeed. They are the confirmed bachelors. Others find 'a' rib, but it is not theirs. Hence it does not fit and causes much pain and anguish. Those, however, who find 'their' rib live happily ever after.

Reason For Scalping

Contrary to general opinion, until the coming of the European settlers the custom of scalping was restricted to only some of the Red Indian tribes who treasured the scalp as a trophy of a slain enemy. The white colonists then copied their example, first in mere retaliation. Soon, however, they inflicted the practice on members of all tribes, doing so for mercenary reasons, as they were paid a bounty for each scalp.

The Red Indians misinterpreted the motivation of their pale-faced enemy. They imagined that he prized their scalps so highly because of some magical power inherent in them. Thus they began to scalp people, not out of cruelty but in the genuine belief that a man's hair was the seat of his strength which, by acquiring the scalp, would be magically bestowed on them.

St Peter's Fingermarks on John Dory

From early Roman days, people have relished the John Dory as a delicious fish. But they were puzzled by the conspicuous circular spots on either side of it. Steeped in religious tradition, they linked them with an incident told in the Gospels (Matth. 17:24-27).

Peter wondered whether to pay a regularly raised (Temple) tax. Jesus advised him 'not to give offence' to the authorities and, whether obliged to or not, to meet their demand. The necessary money would be provided to him miraculously. 'Go to the lake', Jesus instructed Peter, 'and throw out your line and take up the fish that first comes up'. He would find in its mouth a coin which he should take to the tax collectors to give to them 'for me and you'.

Following Jesus' directions, Peter held the caught fish

by his thumb and one of his fingers, duly extracting from its mouth a coin. His fingermarks were imprinted on the fish and have remained there ever since.

This explanation of the spots, which was accepted throughout Europe for many years, accounts for the John Dory becoming known also as St Peter's fish. The Spanish called it *Janitore,* the 'door-keeper' (of heaven), a name by which the apostle was also known and which, according to some, is the real origin of its English description, as the 'John Dory' was the misheard Spanish *Janitore.*

Pelican Feeding Its Young on Own Blood

That the pelican by piercing its breast fed its young on its own blood was a widely-held misconception. The tradition became so established that it was even adopted by the Christian Church, which chose the pelican to symbolize Christ's sacrifice on the cross who with his blood, had saved man. As early as the fifteenth century, 'the pelican in her filial devotion wounding her breast for the sake of her young' became a favourite illustration in heraldry. In 1517 the New College of Corpus Christi, Oxford, England, incorporated the bird in its emblem. As late as 1902 the American State of Louisiana selected the pelican for its seal and, ten years later, for its flag.

The myth is based on an ancient fable which arose from a faulty observation or mistaken identity. A pelican feeds its young by regurgitation. To disgorge the food, it presses the lower part of its bill against its pouch. In so doing, the 'red nail' of its upper mandible appears to touch its breast. Mistaken for blood, it gave people the erroneous notion that to feed the nestlings, the mother bird actually pierced her breast.

It has also been suggested that at one time the pelican was confused with the flamingo. The latter's habit to eject a bloody secretion from its beak had been responsible for the legend.

Lightning Never Strikes Twice

Lightning has always frightened man and, as a 'bolt from heaven', created its own myths. Most prominent among them is the belief that lightning never strikes twice in the same spot. Evidence disproves this assumption. Many well-known tall and exposed landmarks — such as New York's Empire State Building and the steeple of St Mark's in Venice — have been frequent targets.

Another fallacy has it that knives, scissors and mirrors attract lightning. Consequently, during a thunderstorm people either kept a safe distance from them or, at the very least, covered them up and drew the blinds.

Thunder Turning Milk Sour

Prior to pasteurization and refrigeration, people believed that a thunderstorm made milk turn sour. They were mistaken. It was not the thunder that curdled the milk, but the humid weather. This activated a chemical process in the milk, souring it.

Lajipathi Rai Kolli.

8 Common Misconceptions

Misconceptions are not relegated to the past. Equally amazing is the number and diversity of fallacies, half-truths and wrong concepts ruling our lives. Without a second thought, we accept them for real. As we have come across them so often, in fact as long as we can remember, we take them for granted and never question them. Carelessly thus we transmit those errors to future generations. They make up a veritable kaleidoscope of human aberrations.

The Shifty-Eyed Person

It is so easy to misjudge a person. A simple habit of his may mislead people and make them draw wrong conclusions as to his character. A frequent victim is the man or woman who cannot look one straight in the eyes. Condemned as 'shifty eyed', he or she is regarded as someone not to be trusted.

There is no foundation for this 'character assassination'. Some people, out of mere shyness, may look down whilst talking to you. Crooks and con men have made good use of this misconception and, when offering their scheme cunningly — to create an impression of candour and honesty — will purposely look you straight into the eyes.

Obesity and Character

There is not just one type of weight-watcher. Long before man's concern with overweight as a health hazard, obesity was thought to show superiority of character. Shakespeare confirmed this fallacious view when in *Julius Caesar* he expressed preference for men 'that are fat' and decried as dangerous those with 'a lean and hungry look'. We continue to believe in the good-naturedness of the well-padded. He is most trustworthy. Solidly-built, he looks at life and others pleasantly and with good intentions. The reverse is true of the slim.

Reality contradicts this notion. If anything, those suffering from overweight are not the happiest of people. Certainly, they might be kindhearted and good-natured but would be so in spite of, and not because of, their obesity. Apart from Shakespeare's 'authority', a contributing factor might well have been the physiognomy of the stout. His full face covers up folds and frowns, those telling lines drawn by the muscles, often creating the wrong impression of a sour outlook and an unhappy mind.

Platonic Love

By a general misconception, platonic love is divorced from any sexual desire. Purely intellectual, it is supposed to be based on mutual non-erotic esteem between a man and a woman. It received its name because Plato and his school had advocated such attachment between people of the opposite sex.

This totally misrepresents what Plato actually taught. A synonym of *amor Socraticus, amor Platonicus* (as defined in Plato's *Symposium*) referred to the interest Socrates took in young men, also misinterpreted and misjudged in his time by those who could not understand 'pure' love. 'Platonic love', in fact, was exclusively restricted to males, completely ignoring members of the opposite sex.

The Midwife

A midwife is generally understood to refer to a member of

the female sex. The name suggests nothing of the kind. It merely speaks of someone who is 'with' (the Anglo-Saxon *mid*) the woman (*wif*), when she is giving birth to a child. The 'attendant', skilled in the delivery of a baby, may be a man or a woman.

Nudity and Morals

Standards of morality change, not least so regarding dress. It was quite reputable for ladies of Victorian times to expose their bosom. To display their ankles, on the other hand, was unseemly if not immoral, and a show of leg was considered so sexually rousing to men that even the legs of a piano and table had to be 'properly' covered.

For a long time, nudity was looked down upon as depraving, whilst the covering of a maximum part of the body was lauded as modesty. Missionaries were appalled to see natives they had come to convert, running about stark naked. To teach them virtue, they gave them clothes — with unexpected results. By making them cover their nakedness, they roused their sexual feelings, thereby destroying their innate innocence. Adam and Eve in Paradise — so the Bible tells — were not conscious of their bare bodies till they had sinned.

Topless and nude figures do not necessarily express or awaken lewd thoughts. To the unsophisticated, unspoilt by Western civilization, they might have no erotic effect. They are accepted as 'natural', in every sense of the word, and taken for granted. The flimsily dressed is sexually more suggestive and rousing than the nude, as every producer of sexy shows knows only too well!

The Sexy Bosom

The size of a woman's breast is no indication of her sexual prowess. There is no relation between the two.

Homosexuality and Sterility

It is incorrect that homosexuals and lesbians cannot have children. Some of them might be sterile and barren, like any other man or woman, but this need not be the case. They can be as capable of fathering and conceiving a child as the heterosexual.

Hairy Men's Virility

As with a woman's bosom, a man's hair has been misjudged as a sexual 'give-away'. Hairy men are believed to be especially virile, particularly so if they have a hairy chest. No evidence supports this claim. Sick and weakly men have been known to show a thick growth of hair all over their body. On the other hand, the famous Japanese Sumo wrestlers have no hair on their chests at all.

The fallacy, no doubt, goes back to (a misinterpretation of) the biblical story of Samson who, a man of superhuman strength, lost it when, through Delilah's wiles, his hair was cut off! It is interesting to note that even the usual explanation given to the episode does not tally with traditional belief. This did not assume that Samson's power actually resided in his hair. The hair by itself gave no strength. His downfall was attributed to different circumstances. As a man who had dedicated himself to God, thus 'set apart' no knife was permitted to touch his hair which he had to let grow wild. With his loss of hair, however, so it was reasoned, he lost his divine status and, with it, his power.

The fallacy is also linked with the animal world. Men's hairy chests reminded people of the gorilla, that largest of apes. A most powerful animal, it has a thick coat of coarse, dark hair. However, it is forgotten that the huge 'hairy' ape has no hair on its chest!

Hair Pieces

It is not an uncommon practice for bald men to wear toupees, and for women to tint their hair. Hence, things are not always as they appear to be. This applies equally to many a notion on hair.

Growth of Hair

The frequency of the cutting or shaving of one's hair has no effect on its growth. Only warm weather might accelerate it. However, cutting it could make it denser by activating sluggish hair folicles.

Likewise, it is wrong to imagine that singeing the hair promotes its good health. The misconception is based on the erroneous belief that the hollow (tubular) hair contained elements essential for its health which thus sealed off could not escape.

Hair Turning White

That a sudden fright or profound shock can turn a person's hair white 'overnight' is a widespread but mistaken belief. Studies of the structure of hair and scalp proved this to be impossible.

It is true that emotional and bodily upsets may result in hair turning white. This may occur comparatively quickly but never instantly. The sudden shock to one's system may contract the vessels supplying essential nutrients to the hair papillae. Thus deprived, the process of pigmentation of new hair-growth is halted. However, existing hair colour remains as it is. It cannot change all of a sudden.

In the majority of cases, premature greying is due to an inherited trait, though it can also be caused by lack of certain nutrients.

The Highbrow

It is absurd to think that a high forehead indicates superior intellect. Nevertheless, this wrong notion has given rise to the modern 'highbrow'.

Equally erroneous is the belief that a brainy person has a large-sized brain. No correlation exists between the dimensions of the brain and intelligence.

That to eat plenty of fish was good for the mind is yet another old wives' tale. No extra nourishment for the brain is contained in fish.

The Egg Head

The description of a highbrow as an 'egg head' is based on a fallacy. Bald people's heads look somewhat like an egg, and loss of hair was once — wrongly — considered the effect of excessive study and intelligence.

Ventriloquism

Ventriloquism literally means 'to speak from the belly', joining the Latin *venter* for 'stomach' and *loqui* for 'speak'. It is as misleading a term as the art. The ventriloquist does not speak from the tummy. It only seems so. Skilfully he has learnt to produce his voice further back in the larynx than is normal, and to do so without moving his lips.

Man's Five Senses

Since Aristotelian times, man's 'five senses' of hearing, sight, smell, taste and touch were thought to provide him with a total perception of the external world. This is not so. Indeed, restricted to those five faculties, his world view would be very deficient, fragmentary and inadequate.

Man has been endowed with many other senses and, though not having been conscious of them until comparatively recent times, has used them nevertheless. They include his sense of balance, temperature, time and direction. Even these do not cover the whole range of human, sensory perception. No doubt, other senses have not yet been explored or identified. Therefore it would be far from 'common sense' to continue to speak of man's 'five senses'.

Eyesight and Pierced Ears

In some parts of the world people are still convinced that the piercing of the ears improves eyesight. They are wrong. The fallacy might go back hundreds of years to a then popular minor operation, imagined to cure any diseased part of the body. Using a sharp needle, a wound was artificially created in the patient's earlobe, and then made to fester. To prevent it from healing prematurely and to cause it to produce a maximum amount of pus, twine threaded through the hole was repeatedly pulled to and fro. The exuding pus was believed to carry with it the sick substance responsible for the disease. As the earlobe was so close to the eye, people further 'reasoned', the treatment would be especially beneficial to vision!

Eventually, the pus was forgotten and its supposed healing role transferred to the hole itself. To keep it from closing up, earrings were inserted. These were thought not only to maintain good health, but to improve eyesight. Moreover, being of shining metal, they would act as a devil-repellent, as evil forces were afraid of anything that reflects light.

Sunglasses

It is unnecessary for anyone with normal vision to wear sunglasses. Eyes have the ability automatically to adapt themselves to bright light. The pupils will contract to let in less light, whilst the visual pigment at the back of the eyes will bleach. This process, however, is not instantaneous. People unaware of it (or being impatient), do not wait for it to happen. They will immediately put on glasses which will take off the glare.

The only cases in which sunglasses prove essential apply to patients whose pupils have been dilated by the optician for an examination, and to those who suffer from certain eye problems, such as lack of pigment in the iris.

Other People's Glasses

The wearing of the wrong type of spectacles or those of someone else does not damage one's eyes. All it can do is to cause eye strain resulting in a headache and discomfort.

Shingles and Nerves

Shingles were already known to the ancient Greeks. They referred to them as *zona,* obviously because the rash appeared on specific 'zones' of the body. A very painful condition, it has been misunderstood and been subject to various misconceptions.

A popular fallacy believed that if the rash completely encircled the waist, shingles would prove fatal. 'It kills if it encircles', wrote first-century Pliny the Elder.

Even more general is the erroneous notion that shingles were caused by a nervous condition. The mistake is the result of a linguistic confusion. Shingles are an acute viral infection, brought on by the same virus as chickenpox. This affects the ganglia of certain nerves, manifesting itself by inflammation and skin eruption (blisters) along their tracts. Shingles therefore concern 'nerves' in the anatomical sense, but not in any psychological connotation. One need not be a nervous person to suffer from shingles, though suffering from shingles might well make one nervous.

Catching Cold

A cold is so common that people have created numerous myths as to how they can catch it. Wrongly thus, wet feet have been blamed. No matter how wet the feet are, they will not infect the respiratory tract. What might happen is that by chilling the body, a person's resistance is lowered, thereby making him more susceptible to picking up the (still unidentified) cold virus. Standing in a draft in itself does not result in a cold either. Catching it under such circumstances could only be due to the unfortunate coincidence that the air blown into one's face carried a cold germ.

Coughs and Sneezes Spread Diseases

It is good manners for anyone who coughs or sneezes to cover his mouth or nose with the hand, this is meant to protect those nearby from catching the germ. However, this thoughtful gesture may well achieve the opposite result to the one intended by spreading his cold all the same. The hand now carries the germs and might transfer them to others, either by a handshake or by touching a doorknob or tap from which someone else could easily pick them up. A disposable tissue should always take the place of the bare hand.

Breast Cancer

Many women are worried that a hard blow on their breast can cause cancer at that spot. This, too, is an old wives' tale.

Most likely the notion was brought about by the prudishness of Victorian women who were loath to have a doctor routinely examine their breast. If by knocking their bosom accidentally, they felt the bruised spot and chanced upon a lump, they would assume that the blow had caused the cancer, which had in fact already been in existence.

Appendicitis

People fear that to swallow the stone of a cherry or plum or any other fruit-seed may give appendicitis. In the majority of such incidents, the stone will not get stuck, but in the usual way will pass harmlessly through the body, without causing inflammation of the appendix.

On Food

'Do's' and 'don'ts' crowd man's ways of eating and drinking. Many of them are wise rules, based on well-founded experience and knowledge. Others are mere vestiges of ages gone by, and are now totally obsolete and irrelevant. Nevertheless, they are still conscientiously observed. Numerous indeed are the misconceptions about food and drink.

Food fads come and go and with them people's choice of their diet. Typical examples relate to the contrary views as to the value of vitamins and the danger of high cholesterol in both diet and bloodstream.

Green Apples

From the beginning it seems, apples have played a part in leading man astray. Most people believe that the Bible tells that Adam and Eve were expelled from Paradise because against God's bidding, they had eaten an apple. The Bible never specifies the type of 'forbidden fruit'. This might just as well — and much more likely — have been a peach or a pomegranate.

Equally fallacious is the common assumption that the eating of green apples caused stomach ache. Neither the colour nor the ripeness of an apple affects the digestive process. So long as the apple is chewed well, it will make no difference whether it is ripe or green.

Hot Curry

Only those who have never visited India imagine that all curries are hot. There are mild curries as well and they are equally favoured by Indian people. The name 'curry' — from the Tamil tongue — describes merely a 'sauce' or 'relish', without referring to any ingredient which gives a burning sensation. Significantly, the very condiments that make curries hot — such as chili and cayenne peppers — come from the American tropics! They were introduced into India in the sixteenth century.

Tinned Food

To leave food in an opened tin in the refrigerator, so yet another fallacy claims, is asking for trouble. It will go bad in no time. In reality, the sort of container in which the food is stored is of no consequence. Deterioration can only be due to a contaminating agent getting into the food from the outside.

Red Meat

It is merely a matter of taste whether to eat meat well-done or rare. It has no effect on health either way. That red meat was especially beneficial to anaemic people is a fallacy.

Seasonal Change of Diet

Those who believe that it is necessary to eat more in winter than in summer, to 'keep up their energy', are mistaken. Modern heating and warmer clothing adjust the body to the change in temperature, so that there is no need to increase the calory intake.

Effect of Food on Character

It is a fallacy that the eating of meat makes people belligerent, whilst a vegetarian diet results in a peaceful disposition. Both Hitler and Mussolini were vegetarians.

On Drink

Man has learnt to be careful of what he drinks. Whether at home or away from home, he will beware of polluted water. His very caution, however, has led to some mistaken beliefs.

Bottled Water

Tourists to certain foreign countries wisely avoid drinking water straight from the tap. They order bottled water instead. Neither is safe! In fact, bottled water can be more contaminated, depending on whether the bottles have been sterilized or been refilled time and again. Moreover, those bottling the water unhygienically might have added their own germs. There is the further possibility that the so-called 'safe' water bought in a bottle, comes from the very tap so carefully shunned. It is wisest in such circumstances to keep away from water altogether, including ice cubes which, after all, are only frozen water.

Water From Hot Tap

Many people hold the view that it is inadvisable, and possibly injurious to health, to use water from the hot tap for the brewing of tea. There is no hazard in doing so. The fallacy might well have arisen from the flat and stale taste of tea so made. Heated water loses a considerable amount of oxygen, depriving it of the fresh taste of cold water.

Hot Tea Cools
It is pure imagination that the drinking of hot tea is cooling. In fact, the hot tea adds — temporarily — warmth to the body. When this effect has worn off, it makes people feel relatively cooler.

Decaffinated Coffee and Sleep
Decaffinated coffee, really a contradiction in terms, has most of the caffeine removed. Nevertheless, it still retains a minute amount of the stimulant. Even this smallest of quantity might prevent those highly susceptible to caffeine from going to sleep.

Tea and Sleep
Those who cannot sleep after having drunk coffee, imagine that tea will not keep them awake. Unless it is a case of mind over matter, theirs is a misconception. Tea contains theine, as strong a stimulant as caffeine.

Coffee and Alcohol
It is wishful thinking and a fallacy to assume that coffee has a sobering effect on inebriates. As a stimulant, the coffee may exhilarate them and lead them to think that they are less 'under the influence'. Coffee does not reduce the amount of alcohol in the bloodstream nor does it accelerate its elimination.

Mixing Drinks
The mixing of drinks does not bring about intoxication. A person gets drunk not from the variety of spirits he imbibes, but from the total amount of alcohol, once this exceeds his limit of tolerance.

Alcohol Warms
Almost paradoxical is the assumption that alcohol has a warming effect on a cold day. On the contrary, the spirit

dilates small blood vessels and thereby causes warmth to leave the body. It is the ensuing sensation which creates the illusion. In actual fact, liquor lowers body temperature.

Alcohol and Sex

Alcohol is not an aphrodisiac. It might temporarily increase man's libido, but at the same time reduces his sexual potency!

In Vino Veritas

Popular proverbs do not always conform to fact. This applies to the well-known Latin saying that 'in wine is truth' (*in vino veritas*). Its claim that, no matter how deceitful people might be while sober, they will tell the truth when drunk, is a misconception.

The effect of drink varies according to the individual. It may make people jovial or aggressive, happy or depressed. It may loosen some persons' tongues to say things they would carefully keep to themselves otherwise. Thus they will do a lot of talking, but whatever they say may still be far removed from the truth.

Dutch Tulips

Tulips are grown in such abundance in Holland that the flower is generally believed to be indigenously Dutch. This is not so. The tulip originated in Turkey, on the banks of the Bosphorus, which explains its name. From the Turkish *tuliband,* it means 'turban'. The Turks called it so because they recognized a close resemblance between their turban and the flower. Tulips were introduced into Holland — from Turkey — in the sixteenth century. The Dutch then took such a fancy to them that they planted tulips all over their country, developing a wealth of new varieties. This led to the misconception that the tulip is Dutch.

Italian Pasta

Spaghetti, macaroni, vermicelli and other noodle-like pastas are taken for typically Italian. Certainly, the sound of their names seems to confirm the belief. They are not Italian at all but Chinese.

Marco Polo, the famous Italian world traveller had first tasted 'noodles' in far-off China, where 'pasta' had belonged to the people's staple diet for hundreds of years. (Excavations of a tomb at Turfan uncovered remnants of Chinese 'ravioli' dating back to A.D. 800.) Marco Polo took such a liking to pasta that, on his return to Venice in 1295, he taught his countrymen the (Chinese) art of making it. Italians came to relish the novel (and inexpensive) food so much that they lost no time to make it their own, so that the world now gives them all the credit. Historically, however, this is incorrect.

Scottish Myths

Great in number are the contributions Scotsmen have made to civilization. Ungratefully, the world has often forgotten its debt. On the other hand, misconceptions prevail as to the Scottishness of some famous 'institutions', in which fiction has overtaken fact.

The Kilt

The Scots' kilt is not Scottish originally. One of the earliest forms of dress, it appears on Bronze Age frescoes discovered in Knossos on Crete, and used to be worn by the ancient Egyptians. Known already in biblical days, the kilt was part of Assyrian soldiers' uniform. Scotland, in fact, acquired the kilt as late as the eighteenth century.

A foreign import thus, several theories have been advanced, as to who first brought the kilt to Scotland. Irishmen claim that the Scots took it over from them. The most favoured tradition, however, credits Thomas Rawlison, an Englishman, with the introduction of the kilt to the Highlands. As overseer of ironworks in the county of Inverness, he had visualized the usefulness of the kilt for the workers. Scotsmen found it so practical, comfortable and attractive that, in no time, it became their favourite dress, eventually (wrongly) to be identified with their race.

Bagpipes

With their shrill music, bagpipes make Scotsmen's hearts beat faster, and all the world associates the pipes with the land of the thistle. As a military instrument, they inspired the Highlanders in their fight so much that after the battle of Culloden, they were banned altogether with the Highland dress.

Nevertheless, bagpipes are not Scottish. They go back almost to the beginning of civilization and to far-off lands. Bagpipes are mentioned in the book of Daniel in the Bible, and shown on Hittite carvings dated 1000 B.C. They were known as well in Persia, India and even China. A favourite instrument in classical Greece and Rome, bagpipes' rhythm paced the Roman foot soldiers' march. Nero himself is said to have played the pipes. According to tradition, it was the Romans who brought the first bagpipes to Britain, where the English are said to have preceded the Scots in adopting them. Pipes appear on fourteenth and fifteenth century English illustrations of missals and on English church carvings.

At the time, people even made fun of the pipes. One of the carvings shows pigs playing them, no doubt to suggest that the animals' squeals sounded very much like the noise made by the pipes! To add insult to injury, Irishmen claimed that one of their people had sold the first bagpipe to the Scots.

Heather

Even the heather is not exclusively Scottish. This low-growing, evergreen shrub equally covers wide stretches of heath (hence its name *heath*er) in northern England, Europe and elevated parts of Asia Minor. Because Scotsmen popularized their heather, identifying it with their country, it became 'recognized' as their very own. Sir Harry Lauder's composition thus sang of 'Wee Hoose amang the Heather', confirming as it were, the Scotsman's ownership of the plant.

The Home of Golf
Golf, Scotland's national game, is not indigenously Scottish either. Most probably, it came from the Netherlands, as its very name still suggests. Golf is derived from *kolf,* the Dutch for 'club'. The Dutchmen's game of *Kolven,* certainly, had some of golf's features.

The American Fall
'Fall' is taken to be typically American, for the English 'autumn'. Descriptively, it pictures the *fall*ing of the leaves during that season.

However, 'fall' is not an American word at all. It is traditionally English, frequently occurring in the works of the great Elizabethan writers. British settlers brought it with them to the American colony and, whilst the word died out in the Old Country, it was preserved as an English heirloom in the New World, never to fall by the way.

The Jewish Nose
The (so called) 'Jewish nose' is a myth. Jewish nasal profiles are of every type. Jews whose noses are of aquiline shape, share this feature with many other people in large parts of the world, who certainly are not Jewish. The convex curvature of the nose was characteristic of the Hittite people, an ancient Anatolian race!

Jews a Race
To describe Jews as a race is scientifically untenable and incorrect. A misconception propagated by Hitler for political reasons, it has not died with him. Through the millennia of their history, Jews have acquired most varied racial strains from the many people among whom they have lived. Thousands of converts of every race have

joined the Jewish faith, among them entire nations, such as the Chazars on the Caspian Sea.

The Jewish people, therefore, present a wide spectrum of heterogenous racial types. This is shown, very obviously, by the diversity of the pigmentation of their eyes and hair, and the variation in their cranal and facial measurements. That Jews are not a homogenous racial group is further underscored by the existence of Indian, African and even Chinese Jews.

The 'Chosen People'

The description of the Jews as the 'chosen people' has been gravely and ominously misunderstood. It was (wrongly) thought to proclaim the Jews as God's favourites, and superior to others. The concept of the 'chosen people' has a totally different meaning.

The Jews were 'chosen' by God, the Bible tells, solely to be his witnesses, 'My servant', in the words of the prophet Isaiah (43:10). As a people of religion, they were to spread God's message worldwide. It was their mission not to be above other men but to serve them.

This did not confer on, or entitle the Jews to any extra privilege. On the contrary, it imposed on them special responsibilities and obligations. If they failed to observe these, according to Amos' words (3:2), they would incur God's punishment.

A modern epigram expressed wonderment on God's choice:

> How odd
> Of God
> To choose
> The Jews!

Much thought is in the retort:

> It's not
> So odd.
> The Jews
> Chose God!

Expulsion From Paradise

According to the Bible, Adam and Eve were not expelled from the garden of Eden, as is generally believed, in punishment for their having eaten of the forbidden fruit. The book of Genesis (3:17-24) clearly states that the reason was not of a punitive nature, but a precautionary measure. Adam and Eve had to leave Paradise to prevent them from eating the fruit of yet another tree 'out of bounds' to them, the tree of life, as then they would live on for ever, which did not fit in with the divine scheme of things.

Jonah and the Whale

Everyone 'knows' the story of how Jonah was swallowed by a whale. The biblical account of the incident never mentions a whale. All it refers to is 'a large fish' (Jonah 2:1) — without trying to identify it.

The Cooling Fan

A fan does not lower room temperature. It merely swirls the (hot) air around. The movement of air helps to dry perspiration faster which makes people feel more comfortable. Drawing the wrong conclusion, they imagine that the fan has actually cooled the atmosphere.

Colour of Eggshell

The colour of an eggshell depends on the breed of the hen that laid the egg. It is no indication of its nutritional value. This is not related to whether the shell is white or brown.

Criticism as Negative

Criticism is wrongly associated, if not identified with fault-finding or, put the Australian way, with 'knocking'. Such destructive interpretation does not reflect the original meaning of the term and is merely symptomatic of modern negativity.

'Critical' — from the Greek *kritikos* — referred to

objective 'judging'. A critical review can express praise as much as disapproval.

Standing Ovation

A standing ovation is now regarded as a notable public display of respect for a person deserving highest recognition. Hence, it is reserved for special occasions and people of real merit.

The present-day status of the gesture, however, exceeds its original, lesser value. To begin with, an ovation was a second-rate 'applause' and only a minor recognition. The 'ovation' — from the Latin for 'rejoicing' — was awarded to a general who had distinguished himself in a minor battle.

Much more superior to the 'ovation' was the 'triumph'. This described the jubilant welcome given to a military leader on his return from a decisive battle. A major celebration, it included the crowning of the victor with a wreath of gold.

The Old School Tie

The 'old school tie' has played a significant role in English life. It is said that whoever wore it had the key to open up many a closed door guarded by those of a common bond. Surprisingly though, this almost proverbial necktie has been misunderstood.

It is wrong to assume that the old school tie was worn by all the pupils of a particular English public school, such as Eton and Harrow, never to be discarded. The term referred solely to the tie of the 'old boys' who, on graduation, joined a club or an association of former members of their school. No one else could wear the tie, even if he had been to the same institution of learning.

Marriage at Sea

A captain cannot marry a couple at sea. The notion is merely romantic fiction.

Captain and Pilot

It is incorrect to believe that the moment a pilot comes on board ship, he assumes the captain's responsibility. The captain is in charge of his ship at all times. There is only one exception. This applies to a ship passing through the Panama Canal. Even then, technically, the captain has the final 'say'.

Butcher on Jury

There is no doubt that a man's daily occupation must have some effect on his outlook, if not character. At times however, professions and trades create their own myths. A widespread fallacy applies to the butcher. His constant contact with killing and blood, it was said, made him hard of feeling and insensitive to suffering. For this reason, he was disqualified from serving on a jury. This was never the case, not even when, prior to the advent of abattoirs, butchers had to do the slaughtering themselves. No documentary evidence exists of such legal restriction having been imposed at any time.

Turning Clock Back

Everyday speech and popular practice frequently lag behind scientific progress. This even applies to watches and clocks which indicating the advance of time, really should remind man of its changes. When adjusting the hands of their timepiece, people are still reticent to turn them back. They imagine that this might damage the works. They do not realize that there is no need to worry any longer, as modern mechanism allows the hands to turn either way.

Decades and Centuries

A miscalculation advances the beginning of a new century or decade by an entire year. The twentieth century did not start, as commonly assumed, on 1 January 1900, nor will the decade of the 90s begin on 1 January 1990.

A century, as its name suggests, lasts a full 100 years. As the first century started on 1 January A.D. 1, the cycle of a hundred years was completed on 31 December 100. Consequently, the second century could not begin until 1 January 101. All subsequent centuries, to run their full time, must follow suit. To conform, the same reckoning must apply to decades. Just as the twentieth century started on 1 January 1901, so the 90s will begin in 1991.

The Olympic Games

The first Olympic Games were not held in 776 B.C., as is usually thought (and taught). They had taken place many times previously. The mistake arose from the absence of earlier official records!

To call the Games an Olympiad is an error as well. The Greek term was created to describe the four-years interval between the sporting events — a lapse in time and not the Games.

From Time to Eternity

Eternity is one of the most misunderstood concepts. Usually people think that it refers to an infinitely long period. Thus they speak of being 'eternally grateful' and, when discussing someone who has passed away, they say that 'he has gone to eternity', believing that he will live on 'for ever and ever'. It is a mistake to regard eternity as unending, everlasting time — a perpetual continuity as it were, a quantity of years so vast that it cannot be measured.

Eternity is not a quantity but a quality of existence, so different from worldly experience, that no words can describe nor mind gauge it.

9 Wrong Notions Concerning Animals

Discussing the biblical creation story, religious thinkers have asked why God created man last. They felt that it could not be because he was the crowning glory of all that had been made. So they suggested another reason. It was meant to warn man never to overestimate his importance. If ever he became too arrogant, a flea could put him in his place by reminding him that 'Even I was in this world before you!'

Animals have been man's companion from the very beginning, and he ought to know them well. Nonetheless, we maintain many wrong notions and, instead of being the animals' friends, have often looked down on them and maligned them without any reason.

Man has excused his own shortcomings by blaming the animal world, calling all that is despicable in him 'beastly'. Numerous are the unflattering epithets based on erroneous ideas of animal behaviour. You 'chicken out'. Women are called 'catty'. You 'make an ass of yourself' or are 'as sick as a dog'. Nonsensical verse is described as a 'doggerel' and sly people portrayed as 'foxy'. A list of such defamatory language would include the 'hare-brained', the 'bully' and the 'old cow'. You may be 'as fat as a pig', 'as stubborn as a mule' and 'as scared as a rabbit'.

Certainly, in describing human habits and traits there are also many laudatory references to the animal. Conspicuously, however, they are much fewer in number and, at times, inaccurate — not true to fact. To be 'as wise as an owl', for example, may sound like a compliment till it is realized that the bird has very little intelligence!

It is truly amazing how the animal, for so long used and abused by man and often living in such close proximity to him, has been misunderstood. Many are the errors still current about it. How much do we really know even about our own pet? It made the French essayist Montaigne wonder, 'whether the cat is not amusing herself with me more than I with her'.

Man the Only Laughing Animal

Aristotle, like Shakespeare after him, can truly be blamed for the perpetuation of many a fallacy. Certainly, at their time they did not know better, but since the wrong notions were included in their writings, people never queried them. After all, did not Aristotle say so? It must be true, as Shakespeare mentions it ...

Because Aristotle had stated that, 'laughter is the speciality of man', it became almost an axiom that 'man is the only laughing animal'. The Palais Royal Theatre in Paris had Aristotle's passage inscribed above its stage curtain. It seemed so appropriate as the comedies performed gave the audiences so much cause for laughter.

Laughter is not confined to man. Some animals, such as dogs and certain species of monkeys, share this gift. On the other hand, the 'laughing hyena' and 'laughing jackass', the kookaburra, are misnamed. Their prolonged raucous call is merely 'laugh-like'.

Canine Fallacies

Dog's Cold Nose

That a dog's cold nose indicates its good health is incorrect.

Spaying and Weight-Gain

The spaying of a dog (or cat) does not automatically make it put on weight. A weight-gain in the circumstances has a different reason. A 'doctored' pet uses up less energy and therefore requires less food. If, in spite of it, the animal continues to consume the same, but now excessive amount of food, it is bound to put on weight.

Eating Grass and Tobogganing

It is not true that pets eat grass for medicinal purposes, either to rid themselves of worms or as an emetic. The animals might just fancy or need it, as part of their diet.

Equally fallacious is the assumption that the reason for dogs or cats sliding along the ground on their posteriors, is to rid themselves of worms. They toboggan to relieve an irritation caused by a glandular discharge.

A Dog's Loyalty

Proverbial is a dog's loyalty to its master. However, at times this is vastly exaggerated and generalized. Dogs have been known, without provocation, to attack their masters or, ungratefully, to run away from a home which lovingly cared for them.

The dog's repute, most likely, is based on the Greek myth of Argus, Odysseus' faithful old dog. For twenty years it had anxiously waited for its master's return and when, at long last, Odysseus came home, Argus immediately recognized him, in spite of his disguise in beggar's rags. It was a most moving reunion. In welcoming his beloved master, Argus was so overjoyed that he died from the excitement.

Feline Fallacies

A Cat's Rubbing

Cat owners feel highly flattered, when their cat rubs itself against them. They are under an illusion if they imagine that it is meant to show affection. The cat does so selfishly, as the friction gives it a sensuous feeling of gratification.

Attachment to Home

Though cats have been known to return great distances to their former home, they do so only if their love for their human 'friends' who have moved away was not strong enough. Most cats are much attached to their owners and will happily settle down with them wherever they go.

Cat's Hunting Instinct and Food

Feeding a cat well does not stop it from hunting. A well-nourished cat will continue to chase birds, mice and rats though, once having caught and killed its prey, will refrain from devouring it. A fat cat thus has not lost its hunting instinct. However, its obesity may well be of advantage to any potential quarry, as the cat might feel too lethargic to bother or, even if taking up the chase, prove much too slow.

Bringing Home Prey

When a cat brings to its owner a dead bird or mouse, it does so not as a gift, to express its affection or gratitude. The more likely reason is its wish to teach the human what it has learnt to do so well, to hunt successfully.

Caterwauling Sexy

Caterwauling — a term of onomatopoeic origin, i.e. imitating the sound made — is usually linked with a cat in heat or on a sexual pursuit. This is not exclusively the case. The raucous yowling noise may be made by two tom cats when confronting each other, to intimidate the opponent.

The Cat's Night-Sight

The commonly-held belief that cats can see in complete darkness is not correct. However, nature has added to the back of feline eyes an extra, reflective layer of cells, known as *tapedum*. This facilitates the animal's night hunting and enables it to see when visibility has become too dim for ordinary human eyes.

Falling on Feet

A cat does not always automatically fall on its feet. As a tree climber, it is endowed with a highly developed cerebellum, the organ in the inner ear responsible for maintaining bodily equilibrium. At times however, this is congenitally defective. A drop from any considerable height might endanger the cat, as it is unlikely then for 'puss' to land on its four padded paws.

The Pacing Lion

People who watch the big cats pacing up and down in a zoo may take pity on them by interpreting the animals' almost ceaseless movement as an expression of their frustration and feeling of confinement. They are mistaken. The animals would do likewise anywhere. They restlessly walk to and fro not because of being restricted in space. They do so in anticipation of feeding-time or, in natural surroundings, because they are hungry.

Those concerned with animal liberation must beware of anthropomorphising animal behaviour and applying human standards to the world of beasts which has its own rules, lifestyle and body language.

The Thoroughbred

A thoroughbred is not, as often assumed, pure-blooded. The term merely indicates that the horse has been bred scientifically and with great care. Primarily raised for racing, the ancestry of the thoroughbred must be traced back to one of three famous Arab 'foundation' sires, the Godolphin Arabian, the Darley Arabian or the Byerly Turk. In the seventeenth century, these were imported to Britain to improve the native breed. Mated with European mares, their foals were the first to be called 'thoroughbreds'.

The Bear Hug

A tight embrace is called a bear hug. Wrestlers apply the

term to a hold in which a fighter's arms are tightly locked around his opponent's chest and arms. The metaphor does injustice to the animal which has never been known thus to hug friend or foe and certainly does not squeeze anyone to death. A bear kills by striking the victim with its front paws. At times, it might use its teeth in support, though possibly only to prevent its prey from escaping.

Hibernating Bears

Bears go to sleep during the cold winter months, but their state of rest cannot accurately be described as hibernation because the essential elements are lacking. During the period, bears keep on breathing at almost the normal rate and their body temperature is not lowered by any considerable degree. In fact, whenever the weather warms up, bears might well consider, temporarily, to leave their winter quarters to enjoy a spell of sunshine.

The 'Blocked-up' Bear

Erroneous as well is the notion that prior to its winter 'sleep', the animal, especially so the brown bear, looked wisely after the 'lower end' of its alimentary canal. It is a mere fable that, in doing so, it cleverly emptied out its intestines by eating a 'laxative' plant and then used a wad of grass to plug its anus.

The fallacy is based on the wrong interpretation of a correct observation. On occasion, natural faecal matter stops up the bear's anus. It occurs without any deliberate participation on the animal's part.

Goats Eating Tin Cans

Though goats are not particular in what they eat, tin cans are not part of their menu. People who watch (or hear) a goat noisily manipulate a discarded tin can, jumping to the wrong conclusions might imagine that the animal does so whilst eating it.

A goat is not as stupid as that nor is its stomach so tough. Most likely, the goat has found some left-overs inside the tin, and is trying its utmost to get at them. On the other hand, goats like to nibble at anything and, in the process, accidentally discover that labels on tins taste good and give them a sense of well-being. No doubt, this is due to the salt content in the paper (salt being essential in the animals' diet), and the glue which makes them 'high'. Goats had discovered the euphoriant property of the glue long before humans started to sniff it.

The Tarantula's Bite

Tarantulas are greatly feared for their 'poisonous' bite. There is no scientific basis for this. Research has proved that the poison is so minimal that its effect is almost harmless. In the worst incidents, related to a South American species, the victim suffered no more than a rash.

The fallacy goes back to sixteenth-century Europe and its manifold superstitions. People imagined then that the spider's bite could cause vertigo and melancholy, if not death. As the spider abounded in the Italian city of Taranto, it was called after it, 'tarantula'.

Folk medicine prescribed a curious antidote to the threatened consequences of its bite. If those 'fatally' bitten immediately started a very fast dance, their vigorous movement would make them perspire and sweat out the poison before it had a chance to take effect. Primitive peasants soon confused cause and effect, believing that the dance was not the (fancied) cure, but the result of the tarantula's bite.

Eventually, all the circumstances were forgotten and the tarantella survived as a popular fast dance, now totally divorced from the spider. It is hard to believe that it owes its very name to superstition and a combination of fallacious beliefs.

The Camel's Hump

The camel's hump has intrigued man. The animal's power of endurance enables it to exist without a drink of water for extended periods of time. This has led to the wrong notion that the hump serves as a built-in reservoir, replenished each time the animal drinks.

The hump does not hoard water but fat, held in reserve as an essential source of energy for a rainy day. It can be compared to the extra fat stored by some breeds of sheep in their tails.

That this 'ship of the desert' can go without drinking for as long as ten days, is due to an ingenious control system with which nature has provided the animal. As it were, a thermostat automatically changes its body temperature to keep perspiration to a minimum. This checks the camel's loss of fluid to a degree unequalled in any other creature, which considerably reduces its need to drink.

Glowing Eyes

It is fallacious to believe that some animals' eyes glow in the dark. Their apparent luminescence is merely a reflection of light from another source. It is due to the same crystalline substance in the eye which gives the animal better night-sight.

Elephant Fallacies

Thick-Skinned as an Elephant

Misinformation on elephants started early on and has survived the centuries. One tradition, indeed, became so ingrained that it now belongs to our everyday speech. People are said to have an elephant's hide or are 'as thick-skinned as an elephant'. Nothing touches or upsets them.

The comparison is based on the fallacy that an elephant's skin is so thick and tough that it is highly resistant to injury and pain. The fact is that, although an elephant's skin may be as thick as 2½ centimetres, it is not bullet-proof and bleeds easily when pricked.

White Elephants

White elephants exist only in the metaphor, when a present instead of proving a welcome gift, turns out to be useless. In nature, the white elephant is not white but grey. An albino, its only distinguishing features are its eyes which are pink.

Elephant Afraid of Mouse

Almost an insult to the elephant is the myth that a small mouse frightens it. To save the pachyderm's dignity, as it were, some people have suggested that its fear was well-founded, as a mouse could easily get lodged in the opening of the trunk and choke the animal.

There is no truth in this. An elephant has relatively poor vision and probably cannot even see a mouse, though it might smell it. And should a mouse, by a remote chance, ever enter his 'nostrils', a good blow of its nose would eject the rodent fast and far.

Elephants Never Forget

That 'elephants never forget' is yet another fallacy that has given rise to numerous stories, frequently told but never substantiated. Elephants do forget. Though some have a comparatively good memory, to describe the extent of its capacity as being phenomenal, is highly exaggerated.

Use of Trunk

An elephant makes good use of its trunk with which it can move exceedingly heavy loads. However, in spite of the general belief, it never drinks with the trunk. What it does is to suck up water with it which it then spurts into its mouth. Even the elephant baby, when breast-feeding, sucks up its mother's milk with its mouth and not its trunk.

Elephants' Burial Ground

It is a legend that elephants have their own communal

burial grounds to which they retreat when they sense that they are about to die. No such cemetery has ever been discovered.

One of the reasons for the myth is the fact that elephant remains have rarely been unearthed. This can easily be explained. To protect itself against possible attacks from predators, weak and sick elephants will seek shelter in a hide-away deep in the jungle impenetrable for humans. Also, scavengers may devour its carcass, with the bones and tusks eventually sinking into the ground or being covered up by foliage and the growth of the jungle.

That Porcupines Shoot Their Quills

That porcupines shoot off their quills is a popular belief. It has even been suggested that archery was invented by watching an animal doing so. No porcupine ever shoots off its quills. All it does to frighten a foe and keep it at a safe distance, is to erect its 'spikes' (just as for the same purpose it slaps its tail forcefully on to the ground). In the process, loose quills may easily fly off in all directions.

Squirrels and Their Store of Nuts

Squirrels have wrongly been regarded as highly efficient weather prophets. Instinct (or was it supernatural vision?) told them whether the winter was going to be harsh or mild and, accordingly, they hoarded their provisions. Should they gather lots of nuts, a severe winter could be expected!

This is not the case. Squirrels have no meteorological gift. The amount of nuts they gather solely depends on the available supply. They will collect as much as they can find, irrespective of future weather conditions.

Vampires and Blood

Gruesome stories about the vampire bat have grown in the telling. Occult tradition has bestowed on it demonic gifts. Primitive tribes imagined bats to harbour the souls of the dead. Most frightening however, was the belief in the blood-sucking vampire bat. Only certain species of bats, found in Latin American lands, feed on blood. They never suck it. After having punctured a victim's skin with their sharp teeth, they will lap up the blood as a cat laps milk.

The Mistaken Caterpillar

Dr Samuel Johnson's (1755) *Dictionary* made him famous and earned him an Oxford degree. Ever since its publication, it has been used as a reference book. It has supplied valuable information but also been responsible for mistakes perpetuated by the learned clergyman.

This applies to the caterpillar. Misled by its looks, people (first in the fifteenth century) compared it with 'a cat which is hairy' and thus called it in popular Latin *catta pilosa*. Subsequently, its elongated shape made them confuse its 'hairy' part (the *piller*) with a pillar. Dr Johnson adopted the mistake, directing his readers that, correctly spelled, the worm-like creature should not end with *er,* the genuine 'hairy' part, but with *ar,* the tail-end of a pillar. Since then and through Johnson's authority, the caterpillar has not changed its form.

Another suggestion derived the caterpillar from a French root, connecting its pillar section with the French verb *peler,* for to 'peel', 'rind' and 'skin'. Hence, its name referred to the creature's (imagined) practice of stripping the bark off trees.

Centipedes

Exaggeration is not the sole property of advertising. Thus the literal meaning of the centipede is that is has 100 legs, which is a vast miscount. In spite of what it 'says', the ordinary centipede possesses a maximum of a mere twenty pairs of legs!

Bird Fallacies

Hen Laying Egg

A hen never lays an egg. She drops it! The misnomer possibly is once again due to incorrect observation. The fowl may sit on the nest *before* 'laying' the egg or, afterwards, to incubate it. However, she stands up in order to eject it.

To Eat Like a Bird

Whoever describes someone who takes very little food as 'eating like a bird', has little knowledge of bird-life. A bird eats almost constantly. The only time it stops doing so is when it goes to sleep. In reality therefore, to use the comparison would imply that the person referred to never leaves off eating and truly gorges himself.

Free as a Bird

To be 'as free as a bird' is the wish of many. If only they realized that what they covet is a very confined sort of life. Birds observe strictly controlled territorial rights and would not dare go beyond their own area. Any trespassing into other birds' 'airspace' would result in immediate retaliatory action. The freedom of a bird (and its movements) therefore are rather limited.

A bird's struggle for life, indeed, starts early. At the end of the breeding season, its parents evict the nestling from the home. Henceforth it has to fend for itself, an existence that is not as chirpy as the bird sounds.

Bird-Brained

To call anyone 'bird-brained' is not as insulting as it is intended. In reality, it reveals ignorance on the part of the slanderer. Relatively speaking, the description is tantamount to a compliment. Whilst the human brain constitutes 2.5 per cent of the body weight, a bird's brain makes up almost twice that proportion, 4.2 per cent.

Birds' Sleeping Habits

Many misconceptions relating to bird life and behaviour are due to negligence in bird-watching. This applies even to a bird's sleeping habits and the belief that a bird goes to rest in its nest. Principally, the nest serves it for the laying and hatching of eggs. Occasionally, the bird might doze off for a mere 'forty winks'. For the night, however, the bird likes to settle down outside its nest on a tree branch.

Whilst asleep, a bird does not — as is also often thought — tuck its head under its wing to keep warm. What it actually does it to turn its head to rest it, like on a pillow, on its back, sticking its beak under its feathery coat.

The Singing of the Nightingale

The nightingale's name was bound to lead man astray. The bird does not confine its song (*galan,* from Old English for 'to sing') to the hours of darkness but sings just as much during the day. The false impression arose because daytime noise often made its song inaudible, whilst the bird could clearly be heard during the stillness of the night.

Unfortunately, Shakespeare uncritically adopted the wrong notion, adding to it yet another mistake. In *The Merchant of Venice* (Act V, scene I, line 104) he observed that should the nightingale sing by day when every goose is cackling, *she* would be thought 'no better a musician than the wren'. It is the cock which sings and never the female bird.

The Raven

The raven is generally regarded as an ominous bird, an opinion fostered by its jet-black colour, though there are exceptions. After all, the prophet Elijah was fed by ravens when he was hiding at the brook of Kerit, which made the bird in Christian tradition a symbol of divine providence. Legend has it that prior to its abortive mission from Noah's Ark to bring evidence that the Flood was receding, the bird had been snow-white in colour. In punishment for failing to do so, God had blackened it.

Even the raven's name has been misunderstood and linked with all that is ravenous. Ravenous — from the Latin *rapere* for 'to seize' — came to describe the greedy and gluttonous. Obviously, the raven's practice of pouncing on and 'seizing' helpless lambs and other easy prey, seemed to suggest the association. However, the raven's name comes from a totally different source. Its (linguistic) root is the Sanskrit for 'the making of a grating, discordant noise', *ka-rava*. Literally thus, the raven is a 'screamer', a title truly merited by its raucous voice.

Ostrich Burying Head in Sand
That in the face of danger and when alarmed ostriches bury their heads in the sand is a widely-held belief, even applied in daily speech. Faulty observation, once again, is the basis of the fallacy. When sighting possible danger, the ostrich might lie down on the ground, stretching its neck out flat so that it can watch what is happening. It is a clever manoeuvre as standing up, this (largest living) bird would present an easy target.

In fact, ostriches do not always adopt this position. Like any other animal when threatened, this flightless African bird may at once take to its feet and, at the tremendous speed of which it is capable, run the other way.

Ostriches Eat Anything
Ostriches are supposed to digest anything, including iron objects, such as nails, coins and keys. This is not true. Certainly, ostriches are indiscriminate eaters. They may gobble up the most unlikely fare and do so to their own detriment, though pebbles and stones are essential for their digestion. Capable of coping with a considerable amount of foreign matter, too much metal can prove fatal for the bird. Here, too, Shakespeare can be blamed for having

perpetuated the fable. In the play *King Henry VI,* a character threatens his possible murderer with making him eat 'iron like an ostrich, and swallow my word like a great pin'.

The Titmouse
A titmouse has no connection with the rodent. The small songbird's 'mousy' part is a corruption of the Old English *mase,* used in the name of several birds. Misled, people make yet another mistake when they use titmice as its plural.

As Blind as a Bat
Anyone not seeing the obvious is called 'as blind as a bat'. A bat is not blind. A nocturnal animal that hunts at night, its eyes are so adjusted that it sees better in the dusk and the dark than in the full light of day.

Mass Suicide of Lemmings
Lemmings are renowned for their tendency at certain periods to commit mass suicide. As if obsessed with the urge to end their lives, in multitudes they then forge towards the ocean to plunge into the water and drown.

The account reveals a tragedy of errors both on the part of the mouselike rodent populating the northern Arctic region, and men witnessing their 'exodus'.

Lemmings do not want to die. Like any other creatures, they prefer to live. But in so-called 'lemming years', they reproduce in such vast numbers that their food supply proves insufficient. It is then that, in search of new pastures, they migrate in extraordinary numbers. Taking a straight route, they swim through lakes and streams. When, eventually, they reach the sea, they do not recognize it as such. Mistaking it for yet another lake or river, they dive into it, swimming on to a point of no return. A tragic misjudgment in navigation and not a morbid death wish thus explains their fatal plunge.

10 Wrong Notions About the Famous

Fame has its own price. Men and women of renown become public property and — sooner or later — the story of their lives is distorted, embellished or blackened.

Almost inevitably, it seems, they become the victims of wrong notions about what they did and said or what happened to them. The fanciful tales may be the product of imagination or wishful thinking. They also may be the result of ignorance, inaccurate tradition or deliberate misrepresentation.

To examine some of the fallacies concerning the famous is a fascinating study. After all, it is essential to find out, as far as can be ascertained, what people were really like and what they truly said, and how the wrong notions came into being. To discover the facts and to rectify the errors is a rewarding task.

Aeschylus Killed by Tortoise

Aeschylus has been called 'the father of Greek drama'. Reputed author of ninety plays and recipient of at least twelve literary prizes, his influence on stagecraft was enormous. Legend tells that his death (in 456 B.C. at Gela on Sicily) was due to the weirdest of circumstances. An eagle flying overhead had dropped a tortoise straight on to his skull, thereby killing him. The myth was soon believed to be fact and became part of his biography.

Legend further enlarged on the story. Eagles, it claimed, fed on the tortoise. As this animal's strong protective armour made it difficult for the eagle to gain access to its flesh, it cleverly dropped the reptile from high up in the air on to a stone to split open its shell.

Aeschylus had been warned of his imminent death and even been told its date and manner. He would die by being hit on the head by an object. To escape this fate, he went out into the open field. But he could not run away from destiny. He was bald-headed and an eagle flying above in the air with a tortoise in its talons, mistook the writer's shining pate for a stone. Following its usual practice, it dropped the reptile on it. The impact cracked open Aeschylus' skull, killing him on the spot. No record supports the story.

The Hippocratic Oath

Throughout the western world, doctors' code of ethics is based on the 'Hippocratic Oath'. Dating back to ancient Greek days, it controls their professional conduct. Among other things, the oath obliges a doctor never to give information about a patient to outsiders. The patient's well-being — and not his own enrichment — must be the sole aim of his medical practice.

The oath is still taken by graduates of a great number of medical schools and reflects the professional ideals held and taught by Hippocrates, the Greek 'father of medicine' and the most famous physician of antiquity (d. 377 B.C.). However, he never wrote it! It was later ascribed to him, most likely because of his fame. Anything bearing his name, it was thought, would be read and obeyed.

Its present-day text is an edited version of the original — non-Hippocratic — oath. There are significant omissions. They include the promise to honour one's teacher like a parent and, in case of his need, to share all income with him. Should his children wish to take up medical studies, it further pledged, to teach them without charging a fee or making any other stipulation. In another clause the doctor vowed in no circumstances to facilitate abortion or to supply a woman with a pessary.

Nero Fiddled While Rome Burnt

Nero's vanity, cruelty and extravagance made him a most disliked emperor. Scandalous stories about his personal life circulated and grew in the telling. It is not surprising therefore that a man who was so unpopular, if not hated, was wrongly accused of fiendish acts he never committed. It is not true that (in A.D. 64), 'Nero fiddled while Rome burnt'.

Nero could never have done so. The violin did not exist at the time. It dates back to as late as the sixteenth century! Those realizing the anachronism suggested that, if not the violin, he had played the lyre. It is an invented story prompted by the antagonism of Nero's foes. That it gained currency and was accepted as historic was, no doubt, due to the fact that it seemed to epitomize Nero's depravity so well. After all, it implied that Nero rejoiced in the devastating disaster, in which countless victims were burnt to death.

Actually, the emperor was not even in the city at the outbreak of the fire. At the time he was almost seventy-five kilometres away, in his villa at Antium. In spite of it, he was accused of having started the conflagration. Some said that he had done so to create a scene very similar to what Troy must have looked like in flames. In his perversion, it had served him as a most ghoulish background to sing an aria from his own opera on *The Fall of Troy*. Others asserted that his intention was much more practical. He wanted to clear the vast ground of the city, to be able to realize his masterplan to rebuild Rome on a grandiose scale. So far he had been frustrated by wealthy property owners. Nero himself falsely blamed the Christians for the inferno and made their alleged arson an excuse to persecute them.

Efforts have been made to exonerate Nero and to explain the anachronism. Those taking his part claimed that, indeed he had played the lyre whilst watching his beloved city go up in flames. However, he had done so to lament the disaster and give voice to his grief. He himself had taken charge of the men combating the fire and ordered them to pull down whole rows of houses to serve as a firebreak. Later on, this instruction had been misinterpreted as prompted by Nero's warped wish to raze Rome to the ground. The lyre he had played was confused with a fiddle because the Roman description for the 'lyre' — *fidicula* — sounded so much like a fiddle.

Even Nero's harassment of the Christians, it was said, had a valid reason. He had been enraged by rumours that members of the young sect had refused to participate in fighting the fire. If correct, they did so on religious grounds, seeing in the catastrophic event a necessary and expected forerunner of the Second Coming of Christ, which they believed they had no right to delay.

St Patrick and the Snakes of Ireland

There is a detailed account of how St Patrick (d. A.D. 461) freed Ireland from its snakes. Ascending the country's holiest mountain, now called after him Croagh Patrick, he had banished them, together with toads, by a strange ritual. After ringing a bell, he had thrown it over the precipice. With it, miraculously, hundreds of the venomous creatures had cascaded into the depths. Angels then retrieved the bell, for Patrick to repeat the feat until he had completely eradicated all snakes.

All this is a fable, as unreal as the tradition that St Patrick had 'explained' to the Irish the Trinity by means of the shamrock which was thus considered lucky and became the national emblem of Ireland.

There never were any snakes on the Emerald Isle, just as its fauna lacked weasels and moles. Irishmen possibly wondered why their country was free from snakes and attributed it to the wondrous work of their national saint, thereby enhancing his prestige.

Perpetuating the legend, the saint's emblem depicts snakes, and artists portraying St Patrick show him in the act of treading on snakes.

Hamlet at Elsinore

Shakespeare erred when in *Hamlet* he made the king's ghost appear on the ramparts of Kronborg Castle at Elsinore. Hamlet lived before the twelfth century, whilst the castle had not started to be built (by Frederik II) until 1574. This makes Shakespeare's 'encounter' a fantastic anachronism. Even the king's name is incorrect. It was Amlet and not Hamlet!

Dick Whittington and his Cat

The story of Dick Whittington and his cat, though most appealing, is unhistoric. He never was the poor orphan who, thanks to his cat, advanced in life from rags to riches, three times to become the Lord Mayor of London. The earliest reference to his cat, in fact, goes back to a play performed in 1605, almost 200 years after his death!

Richard Whittington (1358–1423) was not born poor. He was the youngest son of a nobleman, the Lord of the Manor of Pauntley in Gloucestershire and, to add to his (good) fortune, married a rich heiress, a knight's daughter. Dealing in textiles as well as engaged in the lucrative coal trade, he increased his wealth to such an extent that Kings Richard II, Henry IV and Henry V borrowed money from him!

The office of a Lord Mayor did not exist at his time. It was established only after Dick's death. However, he served as the *Mayor* of the city, filling the position not three but four times. Dick's fictitious association with a cat has variously been explained. A once popular legend related that a cat had served as a guide to great and good fortune. For people to link it with Whittington would romantically account for his fabulous wealth.

The sailing vessels which at the time carried coal from Newcastle to London were known as cats. The name was possibly suggested by their blackness. As a prosperous coal merchant, Whittington owned his personal 'cat'. Therefore it was quite correct to say that a cat brought him fortune. Later generations, no longer aware of this alternate meaning of cat, mistook it to be of the feline kind.

Another hypothesis derives the 'cat' from the (fifteenth century) French description of profitable trade trans-actions as *achat*. On English tongues this could easily have sounded like a-cat leading to the confusion.

Copernicus and the Heliocentric World View

Copernicus was not the first to teach the heliocentric world view that the sun and not the earth was the centre of the universe around which the planets (including the earth) revolved. His theory *Concerning the Revolutions of the Heavenly Bodies* was published in 1543, the very year of his death. (The reason was his justified fear of public reaction to his 'revolutionary' work, which was bound to lead to his prosecution.)

However, more than 1,800 years before him, the Greek astronomer Aristarchus of Samos (d. 230 B.C.) had propounded the identical notion. At that early date, he had also taught that not only the earth revolved in a circle around the sun but that, simultaneously, it rotated on its own axis.

His view, just like that of Copernicus later on, caused consternation and opposition, particularly so on the part of the established religion. Plutarch quotes a Greek opinion voiced at the time, suggesting that the people should indict Aristarchus on the charge of impiety for putting 'in motion the hearth of the universe'.

Copernicus knew of his predecessor and is believed to have actually referred to his concept in support of his own. However, he is said to have removed the passage again later on, to make people think that he was the very first to have expressed the theory.

Sir Walter Raleigh's Cloak

No evidence supports the historical authenticity of the famous episode in which Sir Walter Raleigh is said to have spread his mantle over a muddy puddle so that Queen Elizabeth should not soil her dainty feet. It was unfortunate that Sir Walter Scott used the anecdote (dating back only to the seventeenth century) in his popular (1821) novel *Kenilworth*. Possibly to give it greater credence, he added that, afterwards, the queen had commanded her (then) favourite courtier to wear 'the muddy cloak till her pleasure should be further known'. The writer's fame made people accept as factual his romantic account of an incident that never happened.

William Penn and Pennsylvania

If father and son share the identical name, there is bound to be confusion. That is exactly what happened to Sir William Penn, Admiral of the British navy and William Penn, his son.

Generally it is believed that the American State of Pennsylvania was so called to honour the junior Mr Penn, the Quaker. That is not so. In fact, it would have been contrary to his very faith in which humility played so great a part, egotistically to have his name put on the map!

The circumstances of the naming go back to a debt — of £16,000 — Charles II of England owed to the Admiral. Penn's son suggested to the king that, instead of paying back the money, he should provide Quakers who were suffering persecution at home, with a tract of land in the New World, to enable them to establish there in freedom a colony of their own. Young Penn intended to call the new settlement either (by the Latin for) 'Woodland', *Silvania,* or 'New Wales'. Charles II acceded to his wish. However, he insisted that the name of William's father should be added. After all, the charter was given to him in payment of a debt. Young William rejected the idea as it was against his conviction. Nevertheless, the king prevailed and it was thus that Pennsylvania (Penn's Woodland) came into being.

'Let Them Eat Cake' (Marie Antoinette)

On hearing that people were so destitute that they had not even bread to eat, only a callous cynic or an insane person would suggest 'let them eat cake'. For a queen to do so would be outrageous. But 'history' attributes this very remark to Marie Antoinette. She is said to have made it on her arrival in France in 1770, when told that some of the population were so impoverished that they had not even bread to eat.

She never uttered the words. They were ascribed to her malevolently, to increase her unpopularity and to justify her later condemnation and execution.

Marie Antoinette was an unlucky queen. Though wife of King Louis XVI, she was looked upon as a foreigner, as 'that Austrian woman'. Disliked at Court for ignoring royal 'etiquette', she was hated by the people for her love of luxury, extravagance and apparent indifference for the underprivileged.

In reality, the phrase 'let them eat cake' comes from J.J. Rousseau's *Confessions* which were published in 1760, when Marie Antoinette was a child of five! Rousseau quotes the words as 'the thoughtless saying of a great princess' (most likely the Duchess of Tuscany) and certainly not as those of the future queen. Even the circumstances under which this unnamed princess made the remark were entirely different. They showed not callousness but compassion. Hearing of peasants going hungry, she advised that they should be given *de la brioche*. This was not cake at all but a superior type of bread, like a bun or scone. Her suggestion expressed the wish to share it with the starving peasants.

The story was a ready-made weapon for the revolutionaries of the time. Taking the passage out of its context, they changed the bun into cake and identified the unnamed princess with the queen. It was a perfect plot to besmirch Marie Antoinette's name and further to enrage the people against her.

Darwin and Atheism

Darwin was not an atheist as has been suggested. The many violent and scurrilous attacks he experienced must have embittered him against established religion as he encountered it at the time. This may explain why, in spite of his many irrefutable declarations of a sincere religious faith, he expressed views which reflected agnosticism and that, on not a few occasions, his wife had to restrain him from speaking harshly against religion. It should give much food for thought that notwithstanding the outrage and controversy his theory of evolution had caused among the orthodoxy of science and religion, at his death Darwin was buried in the sanctified precincts of Westminster Abbey, Britain's holy shrine.

Theologians of old had proved the existence of God from the design of the world. Nothing in it was haphazard or casual. Its very construction revealed a plan and an elaborate pattern which showed it to be the work of a creator. Darwin expressed the identical thought, recognizing the awe-inspiring unity of the universe. The only difference was that he did so in terms of nature.

In many passages — dispersed through his writings — Darwin affirmed his faith, his belief in God, and his practice of religion. There are many examples in his 1831–36 *Journal of Researches into the Natural History and Geology of the Countries Visited during the Voyage of H.M.S. Beagle Round the World.* Thanking the Almighty for the progress of the expedition, he looks forward to entering the Pacific Ocean 'where a blue sky tells one there is a heaven — a something beyond the clouds above our heads'. When he recalls a Tahitian's prayer before going to sleep, he does so admiringly because the native prayed, 'as a Christian should do, with fitting reverence, and without the fear of ridicule or any ostentation of piety'. Speaking of his own crew, he records approvingly how none of them would ever sit down for a meal and start eating 'without saying beforehand a short grace'.

Darwin disagreed with the critics of Christian missionaries. He reminded them of 'the march of improvement, consequent on the introduction of Christianity' in far off places which had greatly reduced 'dishonesty, intemperance and licentiousness'. Darwin said 'It was all the more striking when we remember that only sixty years since, Cook, whose excellent judgment no one will dispute, could foresee no prospect of change.'

When in 1835 Darwin spent Christmas in Pahia, New Zealand, he attended church, joining the natives in their prayers. An atheist could have never written that, 'no one can stand in these solitudes unmoved, and not feel that there is more in man than the mere breath of his body'.

Darwin who as a young man had wanted to become an Anglican priest, could not understand the antagonism his thoughts created. In the final chapter of his *Origin of Species* he thus wrote that he saw no good reason why the views 'given in this volume should shock the religious feelings of anyone'. There was nothing in his teachings to undermine the miracle of creation. Charles Kingsley, the renowned English clergyman and chaplain to Queen Victoria, in fact welcomed Darwin's theory as it gave new grandeur to the universe — 'a new understanding of its mysterious law'. As if to confirm his deep faith, Darwin spoke in the *Descent of Man* of the 'ennobling belief in God'.

Malthus and Birth Control

The Rev. Thomas R. Malthus is frequently quoted as an early fervent advocate of birth control. His name has been so closely identified with the practice that, at one time, contraception was described as Malthusianism. Nothing could have been more inappropriate.

Malthus was greatly concerned with the ever-growing discrepancy between population growth and food supply. A conservative churchman, he vehemently opposed artificial birth control, explicitly stating so in the 1816 edition of his classic, the *Essay on the Principle of*

Population as it Affects the Future Improvement of Society. He refuted 'any artificial and unnatural modes of checking population' as immoral. What however he did suggest was sexual restraint: postponement of marriage and, with it, of sexual relations, till later in life.

The Gladstone Bag

Britain has had many an outstanding Prime Minister. Nineteenth-century William Gladstone (d. 1898) had a unique distinction. No other statesman in the world could boast that, of all things, a travelling case was named after him. The Gladstone bag was not so called because this great leader either invented or favoured it.

Gladstone loved hearing his own voice, and to make speeches was his delight. He seized every opportunity to deliver yet another address, no matter how far away from London. It took him all over the country and the travelling bag became symbolic of his numerous trips. This gave birth to the 'Gladstone bag'.

Gladstone was an extraordinary man with a record in serving his country. Four times Prime Minister, he finished his last term of office at the age of eighty-five, and for sixty-three years — with only one break of eighteen months — sat in Parliament. A bag known by his name immediately therefore also conjured up the quality of durability — like the man himself, it would not wear out.

Abraham Lincoln's Gettysburg Address

Abraham Lincoln's Gettysburg Address, delivered on 19 November 1863, is world-famous. All the more surprising are the false notions associated with it.

It was said that Lincoln improvised the speech, spoke 'off the cuff' as it were. Widespread is the tradition that he had drafted it almost at the last moment on the back of an envelope during his train trip to Gettysburg. In fact, Lincoln had started to prepare the speech, with great thought and care, two weeks prior to the event and did so on official White House notepaper. Though the final text amounted to only 269 words, they were the result of much editing. Lincoln is said to have amended the speech five times! It was certainly not a haphazard effort but a most conscientiously worded address.

Even its exact text at the time of delivery has been subject to doubt. It is believed that the original draft contained no reference to the divinity. However, when the newspapers reported the speech, the President was 'quoted' to have said, 'that this nation, *under God,* shall have a new birth of freedom'. It is possible that on the spur of the moment Lincoln actually added the two significant words, but no one knows for sure. Perhaps they were a later 'edited' version, correcting an otherwise conspicuous omission.

The effect of his speech showed how the unexpected can prove of paramount significance. Edward Everett, one of the foremost orators at the time, had been scheduled to give the major address at this historical dedication of the famous battlefield of the American Civil War as a soldiers' cemetery. His speech lasted two hours. Lincoln had been invited mostly out of courtesy to the President, to follow Everett with 'a few appropriate remarks'. He commenced his address by stating that 'the world will little note nor long remember what we say here'. But the ten sentences he spoke, delivered in less than three minutes, and not the preceding marathon oration, have become everlasting.

Occult Consequences of Lincoln's Assassination

Not unusual is the eerie experience for a lively conversation suddenly to stop, without any apparent reason. It has been claimed that this always happens at exactly twenty minutes after the hour. Americans believe that this coincides with the very minute Abraham Lincoln was assassinated by John Wilkes Booth at the Ford Theatre, Washington, D.C. Like a ghost from the past, the ominous event thus continued to haunt man and halt his talk.

In memory of this fatal occasion as well, it was said, watchmakers using as their trade-sign the enlarged replica of a clockface, set its hands at twenty minutes after eight, the moment of the assassination.

History disproves this claim. Lincoln was not shot at 8.20 p.m. but at 10.10 p.m., and he died only the following morning. The position of the clock hands had never been linked with his death. It was a practical choice to give maximum space for advertising. The hands formed a frame around the watchmaker's trademark.

The Bloomers

Bloomers were not created by Mrs Amelia Bloomer (d. 1894), the American pioneer in social reform and fighter for women's rights. All she did was to advocate dress reform and, while doing so, particularly to recommend the new 'rational' costume which was actually designed by Mrs Elizabeth Miller, daughter of a New York congressman. At the time, it consisted of a jacket, a skirt and Turkish-style trousers.

Mrs Bloomer gave the dress widest publicity in the Women's Magazine she published (the first of its kind in America), and started wearing the costume herself. It caught on and other women, following her example, donned the 'manly' trousers. This created heated controversy. Women thus clothed were barred from churches and threatened with excommunication, which gave Mrs Bloomer yet another opportunity to resume her fight for the novel fashion. Did not the Bible tell that Adam and Eve wore 'unisex attire', the same type of leaf?

All these factors combined to make people wrongly believe that Mrs Bloomer had invented the dress which they therefore called after her. All denials on her part went unheeded. Elizabeth Miller was forgotten and the name of (Mrs) Bloomer stuck, to become eventually identified with women's loose baggy knickers.

Freud and Sexy Dreams

The revolutionary discovery of the unconscious mind by Sigmund Freud opened up an entirely new world. Equally exciting were his dream interpretations. Nothing however exceeded the popularity of his uninhibited discussion of sex and of the prominent role it played in everyone's life.

For the first time to talk freely about a topic so far tabooed, had its built-in dangers. Sex, which for generations had been swept under the carpet as it were, suddenly was worn on the sleeve, eventually to be given an importance completely out of proportion to reality. This created the wrong notion that Freud had taught that *all* dreams were a fulfilment of repressed sexual desires (if not explicitly so, in a disguised, camouflaged form), something he had never meant or taught. Aware of this misrepresentation and to rectify it, he clearly stated in his *New Introductory Lectures on Psycho-Analysis* (published in 1933) that at no time had he put forward the idea 'that all dreams are of a sexual nature'.

Helen Keller's Handicaps

In spite of popular belief to the contrary, Helen Keller was born (in 1880) a normal child, with all her faculties intact. She could see, hear and was far from dumb. However, at the age of eighteen months, she contracted scarlet fever which left her blind, deaf, dumb and without a sense of smell.

Sir Alexander Fleming and Penicillin

There is no doubt that penicillin was discovered (and even so named) by Sir Alexander Fleming, the great Scottish bacteriologist (in 1928). He is also attributed with having established, in theory, the antibacterial powers of the mould from which the drug subsequently was developed. However, its practical application, contrary to a widespread opinion, is not his. The modern antibiotic was pioneered much later (actually when it was

needed most, at the beginning of the Second World War),
by Australian-born Sir Howard Florey and Sir Ernest
Boris Chain, a Berlin-born Jew who had fled from
Hitlerism to Britain.

Sherlock Holmes' Headgear

Almost a trademark of Sherlock Holmes is his deerstalker hat. He never wore one. Conan Doyle did not
mention it even once in the four novels and fifty-six
stories he wrote about the Baker Street detective. In fact,
it would never fit in with the Holmes he created who, as a
man of propriety, strictly adhered to established custom.
Deerstalker caps belonged to the country but not to a
city-dweller.

Sherlock Holmes' cap was his very own, designed by
the detective himself and distinctly differed from the
traditional deerstalker. The mistake can be traced to Sidney
Paget, the illustrator of the *Strand Magazine*. He was
partial to the deerstalker, in which he could be seen from
time to time walking the streets of London. Because of his
fondness for the cap, in some of his drawings Paget made
Holmes — wrongly — wear it as well, and this created the
fallacy!

11 Obsolete Survivals

Redundancy which many regard as a modern phenomenon and the result of technological progress, has been known all through history. Though conditions change and the once fashionable and essential becomes antiquated and useless, thoughtlessly it is retained.

Even organs in our body which, a long time ago, fulfilled an essential role, have become obsolete. In fact, as in the case of the appendix, occasionally they may cause pain and only by being removed, restore good health.

Many 'left-overs' are now part of our lives and, if they do not harm us, at least should be recognized as such, stir our imagination, and make us wonder why man has never seriously tried to update his customs, his lifestyle and modes of expression. It could be said that man continues to pay 'lip-service' to an outdated past.

The Outdated Calendar

Even dates date. But man, as a creature of habit, has made no effort to update his calendar. He might never catch up, not even in the way he calls the months which are now in part wrongly numbered.

In Caesar's time (whose calendar was adopted in Europe early on), the year commenced in March. Accordingly, September was the seventh month, October the eighth, November the ninth and December the tenth. This, of course, is the very meaning of their names — using the Latin *septem* for 'seven', *octo* for 'eight', *novem* for 'nine' and *decem* for 'ten'. When the Gregorian calendar was introduced (in Scotland in 1600 and in England as late as 1752), New Year was advanced by two months. This made the old numbering of months obsolete and inapplicable. In spite of it, no one bothered to correct their names to bring them up to date.

The Birth of Christ

Most scholars agree that the dating of Christ's birth on which our present-day chronology is based, is out by several years. Paradoxically, Jesus was born at least four years 'Before Christ' (B.C.)! The general adoption of the erroneous date is attributed to sixth-century Roman Abbot Dionysius Exiguus who was among the first to 'fix' Jesus' birth on 25 December A.D. 1. There is no indication in the Gospels as to the exact date of Christ's birth. Actually, St Luke's account of shepherds at the time 'abiding in the field, keeping watch over their flock by night' makes it most unlikely that it was 25 December. During this wet and cold season in the Holy Land, the shepherds would have sought shelter for their sheep. It is therefore not surprising that Clement of Alexandria, the third century theologian, suggested 20 May as the correct date for the celebration of Jesus' birth.

The Misplaced Noon

Times certainly have changed and, with it, the counting of hours. Our noon used to be roughly three hours later which rendered part of what we now call *after*noon, morning! Until the fourteenth century, following Roman tradition, the day began not at midnight as at present, but at dawn, from which time the hours were counted. This made the ninth hour, known as 'noon' — from the Latin *nona* for 'nine' — fall approximately three hours after midday, around 3 p.m. our time. When, starting the count from midnight, the hours of day were shifted back, their numbering was not adjusted. Thus we continue to call 12 o'clock 'noon', meaning 'nine'.

The Matinée

One mistake leads to another and, on occasion, in totally different spheres. The confusion of hours left its mark in the world of art. An early afternoon performance is (wrongly) known as a Matinée, meaning 'morning', called after the ancient goddess of dawn, Matuta.

It used to be the custom in medieval times for nobility to have some artistic entertainment precede their main meal on the day, eaten at 'noon', which was then 3 p.m. As this was then still morning, it was simply referred to by that time of day, in fashionable French as Matinée. When, with the change of clocks, the morning became afternoon, the Matinée retained its now obsolete name.

The Good Guy

Familiarly, we might refer to a fellow as a 'guy' and, approvingly, call him 'a good guy'. We do not realize its inappropriateness.

All guys go back to the name of infamous Guy Fawkes, one of the rebels who tried — unsuccessfully — on 5 November 1605 to blow up the British Houses of Parliament. Known as 'the gunpowder plot', the abortive attempt is still annually commemorated in Britain with bonfires and the burning of Guy's effigy.

To use his hated name for a decent sort of person is therefore more than surprising. It adds to the other mistakes which have been associated with the event. Though Guy was only one of the group of conspirators (and not even its leader), traditionally he is made to bear the sole blame. The burning of his effigy, equally, makes no sense. Guy was never burnt at the stake. He was hanged for his crime. Indeed, a vast distance separates the original, historic Guy Fawkes from the modern 'Guys (and Dolls)'.

'Mr'

Most men enjoy flattery and would resent to be relegated to a status inferior to their real position. Recognizing this fact of life and to avoid offence, the practice developed, in case of doubt, to elevate a person by giving him a title of courtesy. If it did not apply, it was still far better than doing the contrary. This, surprisingly, is the origin of our present-date so-ordinary 'Mr'. Originally, in Roman days, it stood for *magister,* the 'Master'. He has been truly reduced in value and cut short, and in his modern abbreviation (in the form of address) has lost all former glory.

The Outdated Mistress

Very appropriately, a wife shared her husband's distinction as the Master of the house, at least in her designation which, adapted the feminine way, became known as Mistress. Everything gets worn by frequent usage, and so did her name. Possibly slurred as well, ultimately it was pronounced 'Missis', though in its abbreviated form as Mrs, it continued to recall her original status as the Mistress.

Once the significant change had taken place, her title deteriorated. Losing its former respectability, it assumed as a mistress (no longer spelled with a capital 'M') the role of a man's kept woman, his paramour.

Perhaps there is a psychological reason for her (mis)appropriation of the Mistress' title. Does not frequently the novel mistress master the Master much more than the (outdated) Mistress could ever do?

As if to recall her past glory, the genuine Mistress of former days occasionally reappears as 'the mistress of the house'.

The Call Girl

The call girl now is generally taken to be a prostitute of a higher class who, well connected, can be reached by phone, then in a dignified manner make her way to wherever she is 'called'. However, this was not the original meaning of her description which has become obsolete. To start with, a call girl was so called because, as a member of the world's oldest profession, she was constantly 'on call' at her communal 'residence', the brothel, then very appositely dubbed the 'call house'.

'*Galled*'

Antiquated medical concepts continue to burden man. At some time, it was seriously believed that fluids secreted by certain organs in excess, changed a person's behaviour pattern. Those, for instance, whose liver produced too much bile, were thought to become rude and aggressive. The notion has been proved fallacious. A pugnacious personality is not the result of any malfunction of the liver. Nevertheless, we are still 'galled' — as an obsolete survival of the misdiagnosis.

The Milliner

Cities have attained world-fame for many reasons, not least because of some product in which they specialized or excelled. Sheffield and Solingen thus are renowned for their cutlery, and Frankfurt and Salisbury for their culinary contributions in sausage and steak. Who would suspect the Italian town of Milan to have found a permanent, though slightly disfigured place in every (English) milliner?

Milan used to be a well-known centre for the making of exquisite ribbons and lace, favoured in the trimming of bonnets. It became so renowned as such that Milaners were eventually identified with the craft of hat-making. When, with the passing of time, this was no longer restricted to them, their former distinction lapsed and, subsequently, was forgotten. Nevertheless, it survived — unrecognized — in the name of the milliner.

Lingerie

There was a time when any direct reference to objects and functions of a 'private' nature embarrassed people. For this reason they chose to describe them by some refined term, a mere hint, a euphemism, or words borrowed from another language, especially the French, which gave them a stylish sound, untouched by any uncouth association.

Wearing apparel, particularly if it was worn next to the bare skin or, more so, covered the body's lower sexual region, became a frequent subject of circumlocution. To give it its 'proper' name was hitting below the belt.

This is the origin of all lingerie. To call women's underwear by its real name, was out of the question. Instead, its French equivalent was used to serve as a welcome disguise, possessing additional elegance. All that 'lingerie' means (in French) is 'linen', derived from the Latin *linum* for 'flax'. As the original nighties and undies were made of that material, the name fitted. Modern society has replaced the linen with cotton, silk and synthetics. Nevertheless and erroneously, we continue to refer to a garment covering closely the female body by the vanished 'linen' as lingerie.

The Blazer

Those wearing a blazer mostly do so to identify themselves as members of a specific school or sporting club. However 'with it' their lifestyle and opinions may be, they are old-fashioned, in fact out of date, in the name of their garment.

A fire blazes away, and a blazer — literally — goes back to a 'torch'.

Towards the end of the nineteenth century, Englishmen's clothes — very typical of the then prevailing British social climate — were sombre and subdued. The only exception were university students who proudly displayed their college 'colours'. Even these, to begin with, in gentlemanly fashion, were rather inconspicuous. It was not surprising therefore that people were stunned, when one day they saw the crew rowing for the Lady Margaret, St John's College, Cambridge Boating Club, wear scarlet flannel jackets. The sight was so unusual, the story goes, that it made even horses shy. Seen from afar, the men seemed 'ablaze', and it is no wonder that their jackets were dubbed 'blazers'. The name stuck and is now applied to all similar jackets no matter of which colour.

A Picnic

A picnic, certainly, is no longer what it used to be and to apply the name to the type of outdoor party held at a site away from home, belies its meaning.

Picnics used to be held anywhere: as much at home around the dining-table as in the open air. The distinctive feature explaining the choice of its name was the combined effort made by all those sharing in it. They 'picked' individual dishes which they brought to the party, jointly to make up the menu. Like so many terms associated with food, the picnic is derived from the French, those masters of cuisine. In their tongue to 'pick' was *piquer*. A *pique-nique,* to begin with, described a small coin or any other minor item. After all, on this occasion as well, each guest was expected to provide (to 'pick') merely a (small) part of the provisions.

It was good fun and, as all shared in preparing the 'table', it was of little cost to the host. Hence, people came to speak of a situation or an achievement that lacked pleasure and had demanded much unenjoyable work that 'it was no picnic'.

Picnics developed into a fashionable social entertainment. They became so popular in nineteenth-century Britain that a special Picnic Society was established in London. Its members met regularly for dinner but prior to doing so, drew lots to determine who was to bring what for the meal.

Added Flavour

To add special spices or herbs to food is thought to enhance its taste. The introduction of the practice, however, was far removed from any such consideration. A variety of reasons has been suggested. When refrigeration was unknown, meat often deteriorated and, to cover up the smell and off-taste, it was seasoned. In addition, meals were heavy and, not rarely, caused indigestion. It was imagined that spices would prevent such ill effects. Finally, in the days when stimulants now served after dinner, such as coffee, tea, liqueurs, brandy and cigars, were still unknown, spices took their place.

How Nuts Came to be Served With Alcohol

The ancient Romans well knew the intoxicating effect of alcohol. They believed that the eating of almonds would counteract it. To keep their guests sober, they thus served them almonds with their drinks, which became an integral part of every party.

When eventually experience showed the futility of the practice, this had become so much of a habit that it was kept on without remembering its original purpose. This explains why bowls of all kinds of nuts are now served at cocktail parties, to be nibbled by the guests with their drinks, totally unaware of their initial 'practical' function.

The Chauffeur

To have a chauffeur driving a car is outdated, not only economically, but in his designation. From the French, his title speaks of a 'stoker', recalling the early days when automobiles were steam-driven. It was his duty, as his name still indicates, to 'heat up' (*chauffer*) the engine. Thoughtlessly, we continue to speak of a chauffeur, though he may drive an air-conditioned (internal combustion) car.

'Outside' London Buses

Passengers trying to get on a crowded double-decker bus in London, many a time are reminded by the conductor that there is room left 'outside only!' With the vehicle being completely enclosed, his words make little sense and, in fact, are bound to confuse visitors from abroad. What the conductor really means to say is that because the inside of the bus is 'full up', all further 'fares' should go upstairs. His obsolete terminology stems from the days when the upper deck of London buses had no cover and its seats were in the open — 'outside'.

Sailing Without Sails

Any travel by sea is referred to as 'sailing'. Even the largest of ocean liners 'sails' to its destination. However, the sails are non-existent. They are carried only metaphorically as a survival of early sailing days.

The Wrong Arrival

Though it may sound strange, to begin with no one could 'arrive' except by sea. The word was coined for exclusively nautical use, as its root meaning is 'to the shore' — *ad ripa.*

'In the Nick of Time'

Scoring plays a significant part in all sports, though its methods vary. In early ball games it was done by means of a tally stick. Each goal was recorded on it by the making of a notch. When, as sometimes was the case, a team won the game by a goal it scored at the very last moment, this was described — very appropriately — as 'a nick in time'.

Scores are now mostly kept electronically. However, the antiquated tally survives, totally divorced from sport, whenever we refer to something as having happened just 'in the nick of time'.

Pens and Pencils

The modern pen completely belies its name which — from the Latin *penna* — means a 'feather'. It is a relic from days long past and recalls the obsolete practice of scribes to use a quill for writing.

Equally outdated and wrongly applied is the description of the pencil. This goes back to the use of a miniature brush which, imaginatively, became known as 'a little tail', *penicillum* in Latin.

Manuscripts and Subscriptions

A 'manuscript' literally refers to a text 'written by hand'. It applied to early documents and was in the form in which authors used to submit their books for publication. Typed manuscripts thus are a contradiction in terms.

A 'subscription' (for membership or a magazine) likewise is outdated and goes back to the time when the contributor used to 'write' (script) his name 'under' (sub) the contract. Literally, he 'sub-scribed'.

The 'Lower Case'

Even when using the most up-to-date, completely computerized printing press, small letters are still referred to as 'lower case'. A proofreader thus will write 'l.c.' in the margin of a galley, wherever a capital letter needs changing into its small equivalent.

The term belongs to the category of obsolete survivals. It stems from the period when all print was typeset by hand, for which purpose the individual letters were kept in containers. While the capitals were stored in the upper tray of a compositor's typecase, its bottom half, known as the lower case, contained all the small letters. Eventually, these became identified with it and, however inapplicable nowadays, are still known as such.

Minutes

A cynic once observed that minutes were kept at meetings because hours were wasted. The mystifying name of the written record of proceedings has no association with time. It goes back to the early days when, whatever was said at a meeting was initially noted down in the smallest possible script, i.e. in minute writing. (Prior to the introduction of shorthand, this helped the recorder better to keep up with the speakers without unnecessarily delaying the discussion.) After the meeting and at his own pace, the secretary then transcribed his early 'minute' script into large copperplate writing. Though nowadays the difference in size and form no longer applies, we continue to keep the original 'minutes'.

A Miniature

It is wrong to believe that a miniature is so called because of its 'minute' dimension. Its name has nothing to do with any measurement. It was chosen because of the colour originally used to produce an illustration or a portrait. *Minium,* the etymological root of the word, was the medieval Latin for fiery 'red lead' — vermillion — the bright red pigment employed in the ornamentation of manuscripts, and particularly so of their capital initials.

As the portraits and paintings using this special colour were usually small-sized, the 'miniature' became identified with something minor in extent, though in reality it had no linguistic connection with anything minimal. People, ignorant of the real source of the term, mixed it up with the Latin for 'small' (*minimus*) and started to (mis)name any small picture a miniature, regardless of whether or not the 'red lead' pigment was used.

Splitting the Atom

Ancient Greek thinkers 'created' the atom. They were convinced that ultimately everything that existed was a combination of most minute building blocks. These were irreducible in size, indestructible and eternal. Hence the Greeks called them individually *a-tom,* for 'in-divisible', 'un-cuttable'.

Two thousand years later (in 1803), the British chemist John Dalton (who was also one of the pioneers of meteorology and the first to describe colour-blindness) adopted the Greeks' atomic theory to chemistry. Applying the identical law, he taught that every substance could be reduced to elemental, indivisible particles nothing could ever break up.

Towards the end of the nineteenth century, however, it was suddenly discovered that the thousand-year-old belief in the indivisible nature of the atom, responsible for its very name, was incorrect.

The splitting of the atom has become a reality. Nevertheless, we retain the outdated concept, whenever we speak of the atom.

To Sum Up

All 'sums' lead 'up' to the 'summit', as theirs is a common root, the Latin *res summum,* the 'highest figure', in every sense of the word. A sum like modern summit meetings at which heads of state meet, referred to whatever or whoever was placed at the very top.

When the ancient Romans totalled 'up' figures, they did so literally: from the bottom to the top, with the final result crowning the column. Though this method was reversed long ago, we continue to speak of the 'sum' and still 'sum up'.

12 False Accusations

Errors of judgment have always been made. Frequently, if found out in time, they were corrected. But in a number of cases they have never been changed. A slander once made, whether out of ignorance or with evil intention, became stuck permanently. However nonsensical and historically wrong, such unfounded calumniations continue to contaminate our everyday life.

The Dirty Pig

Undoubtedly, the pig tops the list of animals that have been maligned and 'verbally' abused.

To call someone a dirty pig or to speak of people as 'living in a pigsty' are accusations based on entirely false premises.

Pigs are quite fastidious animals. If provided with a clean sty and plenty of straw, they will make sure that one corner stays unsoiled, enabling them to keep their bodies clean. Pigs that are dirty are a reflection on their owner who often locates the animals' pen at the worst possible site of his farm, on muddy ground.

That pigs enjoy wallowing in mud because they love dirt also is a false accusation, due to a wrong deduction. The pig's skin is provided with very few sweat glands. In hot weather therefore the animal suffers and, to relieve its discomfort, to cool off, it cleverly rolls in wet mud, just as humans will jump into a swimming pool. Actually, pigs have an advantage over dogs and cats: they have no fleas.

Being Catty

To call anyone who speaks spitefully of another person 'catty' defames a creature that is anything but 'catty'. It is a regrettable example of character assassination in the 'beastly' world. A cat is most 'outspoken', even if only in its gestures and silent miaows. It will never disguise its feelings. Openly, it will show indifference or even contempt to whoever — according to its judgment — merits such disapproval.

A cat can never be bribed nor its affection bought, no matter with how many saucers of cream. Inscrutable and incorruptible, the feline would despise anyone who is catty.

An occasional inexplicable practice on the cat's part may account for the derogatory use of its name. It sometimes happens that a cat which has contentedly been purring on its owner's lap, will suddenly strike out and scratch him or her, the very person to whom it showed so much affection an instant earlier.

The Pleasure-Seeking Epicure

An epicure is now understood to be a person who relishes sensuous pleasure, particularly so in food and drink, in which he is regarded a connoisseur with great refinement in taste. In the very extreme, the description is applied to a hedonist, out to have the best of all worlds, in luxury and in intemperance. Nothing could do greater injustice to Epicurus whose name the lifestyle bears.

A Greek philosopher of renown (born c. 342 B.C.), Epicurus was a most frugal man. He saw as the aim of all existence the achievement of 'a good life'. This, he taught, was attained by learning to minimize pain and maximize pleasure. His pleasure, however, was not that of modern times, with sensual gratification as the be-all and end-all of life. The pleasure he thought of was peace of mind and freedom from want. To obtain them a man must practise moderation and self-control, with a wise choice of food. Epicurus was convinced that one of the major factors preventing human happiness, was a man's 'insatiable desire'.

In spite of the clarity of his teaching, later generations, to justify their own self-indulgence, distorted it. They selected passages that suited them and, taking them out of their context, made the Epicurean synonymous with a glutton and a hedonist, an equation completely unjustified and defaming.

Cannibals

Understandably, cannibals are regarded with horror, as they eat human flesh. However, they are condemned for the wrong reason. Their practice is not the result of a murderous trait, innate cruelty, or a perverse appetite. They do not follow the habit either to show contempt for their enemy. On the contrary, their cannibalism is based on the primitive religious conviction believing that in eating, man did not merely strengthen his body but partook of the 'spirit' of whatever he consumed. Eating the flesh of a foe, the cannibal was convinced, he would absorb his qualities of prowess and heroism, adding them to his own. The practice almost amounted to paying tribute to the victim!

The cannibals' name is an error as well. It is a corruption of the name of the Caribes, meaning 'brave and daring', a native tribe of Central America, still recalled in the Caribbean Sea. When the Spaniards first encountered them, probably unable to pronounce the name, they changed the Caribes into Cannibals. The new name sounded very much like that of a dog — *cano* in Spanish — and, naturally, the people's dreadful custom of eating human flesh was so loathsome that contemptuously the Spaniards compared them to dogs and, as it were, changed a 'brave and daring' name into a canine one. All this is part of the cannibals.

13 Erroneous Interpretations

Many a person is (mis)judged by his physical features, which are wrongly taken to indicate certain character traits. A large mouth thus has been seen as the expression of generosity, whilst protruding lips are supposed to be a give-away of sensuality. A receding chin was interpreted as a sign of weak will and cowardice. The square jaw, on the other hand, was imagined to reveal a determined nature, someone who was tough, resolute and fearless.

Certainly, looks can deceive. It is so easy to misinterpret an intention, a gesture or a facial expression. Body language varies among different people, just as one word may mean opposite things in another environment, even to those speaking the same tongue.

Without knowing the circumstances or certain facts, the conclusions we draw may well be incorrect. Manifold are such misinterpretations. They have been responsible for abstruse ideas, broken friendships and the outbreak of hostilities.

A misinterpretation may have a variety of reasons. These include lack of knowledge, wishful thinking or antipathy. A preconceived notion can make us misconstrue what is really meant and read into words and actions something they do not contain.

A significant feature of Greek oracles was their ambiguity. Their message could thus easily be misinterpreted, and to understand it correctly, at times, became a matter of life and death. Famous is the answer the Athenian envoy received at Delphi when, on behalf of his city he wanted to know how best to defend it against the advancing Persian invader. The oracle suggested that Athens' safety was assured by 'a wooden wall'. Many a war leader would have immediately embarked on building a fortification around the town, in preparation for a siege or attack. Themistocles, however, who correctly interpreted the wooden wall, hastily built up the Athenian fleet, to defeat the Persians at Salamis. It shows the importance of interpretations.

News

News, a popular explanation claims, reflected its worldwide coverage of events: from *N*orth, *E*ast, *W*est and *S*outh. The word was an acronym, made up of the initials of the four directions from which the information was gathered.

The first occurrence of any 'news' in its present-day meaning disproves this assertion, however attractive it may sound. The word existed many centuries before such synthesis was suggested. Not artificially created, news is derived from the Latin *novus,* used for all that is 'new'.

Banns of Marriage

It used to be the law, prior to a wedding to have 'the banns' read out in church. This was done to give anyone who had a valid reason to object to the forthcoming union the opportunity of registering his protest. If justified, the marriage did not take place. (Actually, when first introduced, the practice was meant to ensure that the couple were not too closely blood-related, thereby avoiding the dreaded incest.)

The circumstances and similarity of sound led people to assume that the banns referred to the (possible) 'banning' of the union. This is incorrect. In the early use of the term, the banns did not have a negative meaning. They solely stood for a 'proclamation', in this case the public announcement of intention of marriage.

Bride Crying at Wedding

It is not unusual for a bride to shed tears at her wedding. Generally, it is thought to be due to her excitement and supreme happiness. Overcome by deep emotion, she cries, thereby relieving the tension of the moment.

However plausible this assumption might seem, it is fictitious. The tears can be traced to ancient superstitious fear. In her bliss, the bride was afraid of malevolent supernatural powers which, out of jealousy, would do anything to spoil her happiness. To delude them, she shammed sorrow! Her artificial tears as it were, served as a liquid sacrifice to the forces of evil, to avoid the shedding of real tears later on.

Male and Female

Although the male and the female — as words — sound and look so much alike, one appearing almost the echo of the other, in their ultimate source they part company. One has nothing to do with the other. Each, independently and in its own way, expressed one of the natural and so different functions of the male and the female sex. The 'male' — linguistically — is derived from a root that recalls the man's 'begetting' a child, i.e. his act of insemination. The 'female', on the other hand, from the Latin *femella,* refers to a mother's (role of) breast-feeding her baby. It speaks of the 'milk-giver', 'the one who suckles'.

Chinese Footbinding

A peculiar Chinese custom was the binding of women's feet. (It was discontinued as late as 1911, at the establishment of the republic.)

Practised in infancy when the feet were pliable, it had a crippling effect. Totally alien to western man, he misunderstood the practice and interpreted it as a shameful endeavour to keep woman in her place. Unable to move fast and, as it were, to step it out, she was forced submissively to accept her inferior status. Whilst man could stride along, all she was able to do was to hobble after him.

To the Chinese mind however, the binding of feet far from humiliated and disfigured a woman. On the contrary, it made her all the more attractive. The (artificially created) daintiness of her feet gave her special sex appeal. Were not a woman's mincing steps — even in biblical days — sensuously tempting and so seductive that a man watching her was bound to stumble — sexually?

A Chinese tradition believes that footbinding was introduced through the whim of Li Yu, king of southern T'ang. Watching one of his favourite palace dancers, he suddenly had the idea that her performance would be even more enchanting, if her feet were bound. She gladly obliged and justified Li Yu's expectations. Other dancers soon emulated her and to bind women's feet became a fashion throughout the region. It attracted men from far and wide who, by merely looking at the girls' feet, experienced an intense sexual arousal. If it was exciting to watch the bound feet, to hold them in their hands seemed to surpass any previous pleasure. Far from deforming a woman, the manipulation was thought to improve her figure, making her waist smaller and her bust fuller.

Racial Smells

Racial prejudice has been responsible for many an injustice and misconception. The 'dislike of the like for the unlike' led to the misinterpretation of most innocuous features, to excuse and rationalize antipathies and justify a policy of discrimination. A specific, repulsive body odour was thus attributed to certain races. It was said to make them unpleasant to mix with, if not obnoxious.

The peculiar smell, if it exists at all, has nothing to do with innate racial characteristics. It is produced by certain foods favoured by that particular group of people. Its ingestion causes the pores of their skin to exude the distinctive odour, which a change of diet would quickly eliminate.

Misleading Surnames

There is a story behind everyone's name. To seek it out is an intriguing pursuit. However, at times, one can be misled and draw the wrong conclusion.

Many a family name recalls an ancestor's occupation. This, obviously, explains the Taylors, the Smiths, the Farmers, and even the Chamberlains. It would be totally erroneous for a Mr King, Duke or Prince, in like manner, to imagine that they were descendants from royalty, as suggested by their names. In their case, these go back to completely different circumstances. In medieval times, many cities held annual pageants or processions in which, on each occasion, members of the same family came to personify the identical figure, such as that of the king, the prince or the duke. At first, this was done for a merely practical reason. They had learnt the role and, hence, there was no need for them in the following year to study a new part. It also enabled them to make their performance ever more real and true to the nature of the character they portrayed.

With the passing of time, the family came to regard the specific role as their prerogative. Eventually, they were identified with it, and that is how so many Kings, Dukes and Princes survive. Their original home was not a castle or a palace, but the stage.

This also explains the otherwise puzzling phenomenon of families bearing the name of Pope, Bishop or Priest. No one could (legitimately) ever have descended from them as, of course, their very status implied celibacy. People so called, can be sure that their 'titled' name was not inherited from an ancestor who filled the ecclesiastical office, but from play-acting.

The Illiterate 'X'

It was not exclusively illiteracy that made the cross the

signature of those who could neither read nor write. In such cases, any other mark, a circle, square or simple tick, could have served the same purpose. Even literate and learned men who could well have signed their name, often substituted it with the cross. Its choice therefore must be of a totally different nature.

There have always been dishonest people who would sign well nigh anything, false or true, so long as it was to their advantage. However, at a time when religion still dominated life, they would have been too scared to make use of a sacred symbol to deceive others. Hence, in a Christian society, they would never place the sign of the sacred cross as their signature under something they knew to be untrue. The 'cross' thus ensured the absolute veracity of the statement it endorsed or the fulfilment of any promise made in the document. This was the original purpose of the so-called illiterate 'cross'.

The Symbol of Silence

The placing of the index finger in front of one's mouth is the universally accepted gesture to invite silence. It speaks more loudly than words could do. However, this interpretation is based on an early misunderstanding. The sign goes back to the ancient Egyptians' worship of the child-god Horus, son of the goddess Isis. Traditionally, he was depicted as an infant who, very humanly, was sucking his finger. The Greeks did not recognize the portrayal for what it was, but mistook the simple childish habit as a divine indication of silence. Subsequently, their error, undetected, was adopted throughout Europe, later on to be rationalized as a symbolic sealing of one's lips.

Nightmares

Nightmares have terrified people so much that their experience has left its mark even as a figure of speech. Confusing indeed, their name has been misinterpreted. Its 'mare' part has nothing to do with a female horse. It goes back to ancient superstition and the belief in an evil spirit, known as 'mare'. Also described as *incubus*, it visited people in their sleep and, settling on their chest like a heavy weight, harassed them, producing in their victim a sensation of suffocation.

Belief in this mare has long been discarded, which explains why people no longer connect the (night)mare with the world of the occult, but wrongly see in it the mysterious presence of an equestrian creature.

Jack Tar

Before sailors learnt to protect themselves against the wet with oilskins, they used to coat their canvas clothing with tar, achieving the same result. This, it is often wrongly claimed, explains their description as Jack Tar, also interpreted as the shortened version of their *tar*paulin.

Actually, the name goes back to much earlier days, when all sailing boats were built of timber. To keep them waterproof and seaworthy, they had to be regularly caulked and tarred. In fact, each time a boat was tied up in port, it became the duty of sailors to undertake this task. In the process the tar got stuck to their hands and faces and, hard to remove, soon became their mark of identification responsible for their nickname.

Sailor's Three Stripes

The three stripes on the collar of English naval personnel has caused much speculation. However, the usual explanation that the stripes were introduced to recall Lord Nelson's three great naval victories, is incorrect.

The stripes are merely decorative. They have no historical association. Indeed, they are not confined to members of the British navy, but could equally be found on the collars of American and German naval men. Significantly, the stripes adorned the collars of French sailors as well, many years prior to the British Admiral's three famous battles.

To begin with, the wearing of uniforms was not a general rule in the British navy. It became only obligatory in the eighteenth century, and even then was restricted to officers. It took another 100 years before the regulation was applied to ratings. To achieve complete uniformity, a special naval committee was appointed in 1856. Their deliberations included the sailor's collar which, at the time, still varied, displaying either two or three white stripes.

It was agreed to limit their number to two. But someone made a mistake and, when the new regulation was published, contrary to the decision, this stipulated that the collar of naval men should carry three white stripes. The error has never been rectified.

The Landlubber

To refer to people as landlubbers is taken to express sailors' contempt for those not at home at sea. Their *love* of the land made them long to be back on shore. This explanation misinterprets the 'lubber' to mean a 'lover'. However, there is no relationship between the two. From a Scandinavian root, 'lubber' describes a 'clumsy' sort of person who, lacking experience, is good for nothing and would be as awkward and incapable on land as at sea.

SOS

SOS, the universally adopted distress signal, is generally believed to stand for '*S*ave *O*ur *S*ouls'. This would imply that the sailors' bodies were lost already! Others have seen in the call an abbreviation of '*S*ave *O*ur *S*hip'. Neither interpretation is correct. The choice of the letters has no connection with any verbal message. They were selected because SOS in Morse code — three dots, three dashes, three dots — was most easy to transmit and to be recognized. No special training was needed to make or understand the emergency call.

The Tram

It has been suggested that the tram was so called to honour a person, though opinions differ as to whom.

According to some it was named after Sir James Ou*tram* (d. 1864). He was a renowned British army commander in India whose brilliant military exploits had made him a famous and popular figure at the time, well meriting public recognition. Another less martial and noble derivation traces the (name of the) tram to a Benjamin Ou*tram*. He owned a quarry in the English county of Derbyshire. This claim is not as far-fetched as it may appear, if it is realized that the earliest trams were not used to transport people but to move coal from mines and stones from quarries.

Actually, the 'tram' is of a much earlier origin and goes back to at least 1555. Its description is not the (truncated) name of any Englishman, but refers to one of the significant features of the trucks which were the immediate forerunners of modern trams. To facilitate their movement along the often uneven and difficult ground near the mine or quarry, they ran on rails. Initially, these were wooden beams, known as *traam* in Old German. The 'cars' were called after them. Unfortunately, along the way, people forgot where the tram really came from and, interested to know not only its destination but also its origin, derailed it, as it were.

Whistling Backstage

Not all superstitions, initially, were irrational. Many were precautionary measures against bad luck, brought about not by mysterious demonic forces but by human negligence or untoward accidents. This applies to some well-known theatrical superstitions which do not reflect actors' feelings of insecurity, but recall some unfortunate incident they want to prevent from recurring.

A strictly adhered to taboo concerns whistling backstage. It was misinterpreted as whistling up the devil who, always eager and ready to do mischief and spoil success, would ruin the performance. Should, inadvertently, an actor forget himself and whistle, he had to follow conscientiously a prescribed ritual to counteract any possible harmful effect. Leaving the room, he had humbly to ask to be readmitted and utter a string of profanities.

The true reason was well founded on common sense. During the eighteenth and nineteenth centuries, it was the practice to give stage-hands their instructions not by word of mouth but by a variety of whistles. Their number told them whether to move scenery, to lower or raise stage props or even to open up a trap-door. Any other 'whistle' could easily be mistaken, leading to confusion and serious accidents.

Fresh Flowers Unlucky on Stage

The presence of real flowers on stage is thought to be unlucky. This is not a mere superstition, but based on practical considerations.

Gas lamps, once used to light up the theatre, generated heat which made flowers wilt quickly, with the result that their petals and leaves dropped to the ground, presenting a hazard to unwary actors. To be kept fresh, cut flowers had to be placed into a vase of water. This could easily be upset and the water spilled, causing actors to slip. Some players, allergic to fresh flowers, could suffer a bout of hayfever, spoiling the performance. Also, as fresh flowers had constantly to be replaced, an unnecessary expense would be added to an already tight budget. All these factors combined, were responsible for the not so superstitious 'superstition'.

A Cat's Lick

Cat lovers like to think that when their cat licks their hand or any other bare part of their body, it does so to show affection. However, to see in a cat's lick a kind of feline kiss misinterprets its reason which is far removed from any expression of love. Like humans, at times cats need salt and having discovered its presence on their owner's skin try to lick it off. Their own well-being thus and not love is the motive.

Sourpuss

A sourpuss is not related to a cat. The 'pussy' part is American slang for a 'face'. Derived from the Irish *pus* for a 'mouth', it seems a most appropriate choice of word. The turned-down corners of a person's mouth reflect his sour disposition. Never smiling, he presents a gloomy mien, scowling and morose.

To Curry Favour

Whoever seeks to gain special advantage by excessively flattering an influential person is said 'to curry favour'. Though the meaning of the phrase is clear, its origin has been misunderstood. It is rarely realized that the expression was born in the stable!

The 'favour' in this case is the corrupted name of Favel (or Fauvel), a legendary chestnut mare and subject of a fourteenth-century French satire. Highly prized, she was well looked after. To curry, a term also derived from the French and in no way connected with Indian curry, described the grooming and rubbing down of a horse, a meaning still recalled in the curry comb used for this purpose. 'To curry Favel' therefore expressed the special care and concern shown to the horse.

When, eventually, the English adopted the phrase, they misunderstood and distorted the French, rendering it in their tongue 'to curry favour'. Thus the metaphor became totally divorced from its original equestrian context.

The Kangaroo

The kangaroo, so a story is told, hopped into our vocabulary by misinterpreting something that was said. When the early explorers first encountered the marsupial, they had not the faintest idea what it was. Anxious to know the animal's name, one of the men is said to have asked an Aborigine who happened to stand nearby, 'Can you tell me what it is called?' The native was highly amused by the English so foreign to him, and mimicked the questioner. His imitation produced a sound very much akin to kangaroo. The Englishman, not realizing on his part that the Aborigine was merely aping his question, imagined that he had actually answered it and that 'kangaroo' was the Australian name of the marsupial.

A slightly different version, equally discarded as mere fiction, claims that Joseph Banks had asked the question. The Aborigine had replied, 'I don't know', something like 'kangaroo' in his dialect. The naturalist had mistaken this for the name of the animal.

Even more far-fetched is another explanation. This links the kangaroo's name with the tradition that Australian Aborigines were survivors of the Ten Lost Tribes of Israel. They had given the animal an ancient Hebrew description, *kahn-gahroo,* recalling that 'here they dwelt'. Out of it has sprung the kangaroo!

An Eye For an Eye

'An eye for an eye' has often been condemned as a principle of revenge. This completely misinterprets the intention of the Hebrew axiom, taking it out of its historical context. The law aimed not at ruthless retaliation, but at establishing a system of dispassionate justice in a world of blood feuds, vendettas and wild vengeance.

When the law was first promulgated, society was divided into classes and punishment meted out according to the status of both victim and culprit. For instance, if anyone considered inferior had inflicted bodily harm on a man of superior standing, the punishment never fitted, but by far exceeded the crime.

The principle of 'an eye for an eye' therefore for the first time ever introduced one type of justice for all, irrespective of the individual's social position. More significantly, it limited punishment to its right proportions, was equitable and removed from hatred.

To make the new kind of advanced justice clear to everyone, the Hebrew Bible used not general terms but telling examples. They could easily be understood by everyone. That is why it ruled, 'one eye for an eye, one tooth for a tooth, one hand for a hand ...' When Augustine, one of the early Fathers of the Church, discussed the passage, he remarked on this notable development in which the pagans' unbounded lust for revenge was replaced by the Hebrew concept of a righteous world, 'One eye, not two, for an eye; one tooth, not ten, for a tooth; one life, not the whole family, for a life; and the tooth of a poor man must be regarded as precious as that of the rich'.

Actually, the injunction was never literally applied which, in any case, would have been a practical impossibility. From early days, Jewish authorities interpreted the passage to refer to monetary compensation, in which the guilty party had 'to pay for the crime', the amount of the fine carefully to be determined by an impartial judge.

The Rich and The Eye of a Needle

Much thought has been given to Jesus' observation that it was easier for a camel to go through a needle's eye than for a rich man to enter the kingdom of God (Matth. 19:24).

The metaphor seemed so far-fetched, if not absurd that many authorities came to the conclusion that Jesus had never used it. He was misquoted, they said, because of a scribe's error. They suggested that the original (Greek) text of the Gospel never mentioned a camel but, instead, a thick rope or a cable, which would make sense. For a rich man to go to heaven, Jesus had said, was more difficult than to thread a thick rope through the eye of a needle. The confusion between the rope and the camel could easily be explained, as in the Greek language 'camel' and 'needle' were so much alike, both in spelling and sound. The one was *kamelos* and the other *kamilos*.

Another interpretation made Jesus refer not to a needle or its eye, but to one of the gates in the wall surrounding Jerusalem. This was so low and narrow that it was difficult even for pedestrians to pass through it. For a camel to do so was well nigh impossible. Very appropriately thus, the gate became popularly known as 'the eye of a needle'. It served Jesus as a most fitting illustration to drive home his message.

Both explanations however may well be wrong. In his parables Jesus liked to employ metaphors that were so striking that they immediately caught people's attention and would not be forgotten. He also frequently used idioms and figures of speech current at the time, quoting favourite rabbinical sayings. A very similar metaphor, used to underscore the absurdity of an impossible task, occurs in contemporary Hebrew writings. This spoke of 'an elephant passing through the eye of a needle'. No doubt, Jesus knew this simile. Adapting it to local conditions, he replaced the elephant by the almost equally large camel, an animal well known in Jerusalem.

Jesus was not an antagonist of the rich, and any such deduction from the passage would further misinterpret it. What he intended to say was that money could never buy salvation. A rich man who imagined that his wealth could save him, was gravely mistaken.

Selah

Selah is generally taken to be an almost sacrosanct Hebrew word which, interspersed in the Psalms, is pronounced with great reverence. It has baffled translators, some of whom have — mistakenly — rendered it 'for ever and always'.

In reality, 'Selah' is untranslatable. A simple musical term, it directed the leader of the ancient Temple orchestra to stop the choir from singing, for the instrumentalists to start playing an interlude and doing so with increased volume, possibly produced by the clashing of cymbals and a fanfare of trumpets.

To read out the word Selah as part of the text, as is the present-day practice, therefore is wrong.

Exception Proves the Rule

That 'exception proves the rule' is a maxim frequently quoted to assert that, in spite of contradictory evidence, an accepted norm is still valid. It is a misinterpretation, as one of the decisive words in the phrase has changed in meaning. To 'prove' anything now means to confirm. This was not the original sense of the word.

'Proving' is derived from the Latin *probare,* responsible also for 'probate' and 'probation'. The term initially referred to a process of probing, testing and examining. Very appropriately and logically therefore, an exception to a general rule *tested* its validity. It did not demonstrate it.

This explains, too, the otherwise rather odd observation that 'the *proof* of the pudding is in the eating'. What it means to say is that only by tasting the pudding do we test it and find out what it is like.

The Last Inn

At times, a name seems just to ask to be misunderstood. Certainly, this applies to a public house in the Welsh seaside resort of Barmouth. Called 'The Last Inn', it led people to believe that no other tavern could be found on that road further along and that — as in the case of garages — it would be wise to 'fill up' there, whether with a snack or some drink.

In reality, however, there is nothing final in that inn. Its 'last' refers to the wooden or metal form on which cobblers make or mend shoes. In fact, the sign hanging outside 'The Last Inn' portrayed a shoe placed on a last. Undoubtedly, 'The Last Inn' was once either a favourite spot for cobblers to meet in or, more likely, a cobbler's place of work. People coming to have their shoes repaired, whilst waiting for the job to be done, could spend the time enjoyably by having a pint or two.

14 Mistranslations Perpetuated — With at Times Serious Consequences

The vocabulary of any language has its difficulty. The same word may describe completely different ideas because various roots have become blended in it. Specific local circumstances may have given a phrase or term emotional associations, which just cannot be felt in any other tongue. For the proper understanding of a passage therefore, the mere use of a dictionary is insufficient. This explains why official translators are known as interpreters. All they can do is to try to interpret the meaning of what has been said or written in another language. Their translations are approximations.

The occurrence of mistranslations thus is not a surprising phenomenon. Not necessarily because of any inadequacy on the part of the translator, it may well be the result of the lack of equivalent terms in the other tongue. There are cases however, in which the mistranslation was not an innocuous error but purposely done: to please, to avoid unpleasant consequences, or to defame and denigrate. Mistranslations have played a significant and, at times, tragic role in the history of man.

The Adam's Apple
Adam's apple is the popular description of the odd protrusion in man's throat, caused by the thyroid cartilage of the larynx. Legend tells that it is a piece of the forbidden fruit Adam ate. It became permanently stuck in his throat, as a constant reminder of man's first sin.

As the Bible never identified the 'forbidden fruit' as an

apple, its 'preservation' in the Adam's apple is all the more surprising. It is due to an early misconception.

To begin with, anatomists named this bulge in man's throat very factually *pomum viri*. *Pomum* was the general (Latin) description of anything that was rounded in shape and therefore well suited for that 'lump'. *Vir* (which gave us our 'virility') was the Latin for 'man'. Its Hebrew and Arab equivalent was *adam* which made early doctors refer to *pomum viri* as *pomum adami*.

As an apple was spherical in shape, it, too, was described as *pomum*. This misled even the learned who, confusing the two, imagined that *pomum adami* meant 'Adam's apple'. The twice non-existent fruit was thus (wrongly) perpetuated in popular anatomy.

Helpmate

The first 'helpmate' arrived by mistake. When God created woman, the Bible tells, he did so because he felt that it was not good for man to be alone. Obviously, any companion he was to provide, had to be 'suitable'. When the Hebrew text was translated into English, in the idiom of the time, God is quoted to have said that 'I will make him a help *meet* ("suitable") for him'. Later generations, unaware of the original sense of *meet,* misunderstood the quotation, changing help meet into 'helpmate', and woman, meant from the very beginning as it were to be on par with man — through a linguistic error — was demoted, to become a mere auxiliary and supporter.

Joseph's Coat of Many Colours

Joseph's 'coat of many colours' (Gen. 37:3) has puzzled people. It just did not make sense that a garment, merely because of its colourfulness, should have aroused such envy in Joseph's brothers that they 'could not speak a friendly word to him'.

The fact is that the 'many colours' are not mentioned in the original text. They, too, are based on a mistranslation of a single word, the Hebrew *passim*. This did not refer to any multiplicity of colours, but to the coat's extra-ordinary length: both in hemline and sleeves. Such a garment was not worn by the working man. The 'long tunic with sleeves' indicated authority. Conspicuously it placed its wearer among the leisured and ruling class. It was no wonder therefore that Joseph's brothers showed deep resentment when their father thus singled out young Joseph and thereby elevated him above them.

What happened is obvious. When the Bible was first rendered into Aramaic and Greek, the translators were not certain what the word *passim* meant. They merely guessed that it referred to some 'variation': a 'special' coat which was either multicoloured or made up of strips of cloth of many hues. Subsequent translators of the Bible did not query this interpretation but adopted it, which made the 'coat of many colours' part of our linguistic heritage and biblical lore. And all this is due to a mistake!

The Horned Moses

One of the most famous statues of Michelangelo is his *Horned Moses*. Now standing in the Roman Church of St Pietro in Vincoli, it has been the subject of much speculation. People wondered what had prompted the sculptor to give Moses horns.

Several explanations have been given. Some saw in the horns simply the fancy of Michelangelo's genius. Others considered them symbolic of Moses' spiritual force, a materialization of the divine light that inspired him. More critical scholars pointed to obvious parallels in pagan mythology, the horned representation of Babylonian and Egyptian deities, and claimed that Michelangelo had copied them. They also quoted a passage from the Koran in which Alexander the Great was called the 'two-horned', which suggested that the horns expressed authority and power.

Yet none of these answers is correct. Neither a super-natural miracle nor the adoption of pagan tradition was responsible for Moses' horns. They are the result of a mistake, of one misunderstood word in the Hebrew Bible.

Pitfalls exist in all languages. They are multiplied in Hebrew because its ancient text lacked vowels. It was left to the reader's scholarship to add these to the skeleton of consonants. As an illustration, this could be compared to an English word represented solely by the three consonants BRD. Only the context and erudition on the part of the reader would be able to determine whether these stood for a bird, a bard, a beard or bread, to quote only a few possibilities.

When the Bible describes how Moses, for the second time, came down from Mount Sinai, carrying the tablets of the Law inscribed with the ten commandments, it tells that, 'Moses knew not that his face KRN'. In Hebrew the combination of the three consonants KRN can have two totally different meanings, either 'to shine' or 'to sprout horns'. (Actually, it was the latter which formed the root of the Greek *keras,* the Latin *cornu* and the English *horn,* all of which developed from the Hebrew KRN.)

Jewish tradition and the fact that further on in the passage we are told that Moses had to cover his face with a veil, leave no doubt as to the correct word. It could only be that his face 'shone'. In the exaltation of the moment, he was radiant. It was as if a supernatural light emanated from his inspired countenance. Indeed, so strong was the light that the people were afraid to approach him.

Yet the word was misunderstood and the wrong alternative chosen. It was perhaps because of his pagan background that Aquila, a second-century convert to Judaism, when translating the Hebrew Bible into Greek, rendered KRN as 'sprouted horns'. The (later) Latin translation of the Bible, the Vulgate, which in the sixteenth century became the official Roman Catholic version, copied this error, interpreting the word to mean *cornuta erat.* As a devout Catholic, Michelangelo used the text approved by his Church, and thus created his 'Horned Moses', a unique piece of art, but distinguished even more for its perpetuation in stone of an early translator's mistake.

'Love Your Neighbour'

One of the best-known and most frequently quoted commandments of the Hebrew Bible (Lev. 19:18) is generally mistranslated as, 'You shall love your neighbour *as yourself.'* Correctly rendered it should say, 'You shall love your neighbour *for he is as you are.'* There is a world of difference between the two. The faulty translation puts man's ego first. Condescendingly, it assures our fellow human being that 'I love you as much as I love myself.' Properly translated, the passage emphasizes the sameness of all men who, as equals, are entitled to each other's love.

'The Apple of The Eye'

It is a strange phenomenon that even the most fervent atheist cannot get away from the Bible. Its text has become so interwoven with western culture that — without our knowing — we quote from Scripture at least as much as from Shakespeare. To cherish anyone like 'the apple of the eye' is a biblical metaphor, though, unfortunately, the result of yet another of its mistranslations. It is quoted as a simile to describe God's care for Israel who was as precious to him 'as the apple of the eye'.

The original Hebrew text however does not mention the apple at all. Instead, it simply speaks of the 'pupil' of the eye (Dt. 32:10). It was a well-chosen comparison, as this most treasured part of the organ of vision, if damaged, could cause blindness. Hence, it needed special care.

In the early days, it was erroneously assumed that the pupil was a solid, spherical body, very much like an infinitesimally small 'apple'. This misconception introduced the 'apple of the eye', a mistake that has never been discarded.

Black Art

A mistranslation gave us 'black art' which, to make it even more absurd, came from the dead. It all started in the ancient belief that the future could be revealed to man by his communicating with those who had passed away. From beyond the grave, they could see — and tell — what lay ahead. Among the Greeks this occult pursuit became known as necromancy, joining their words for 'dead' (*nekros*) and 'prophecy' (*manteia*). In later years and foreign climes, the term was much too learned and complex to be understood by the ordinary people, still anxious to know what was going to happen to them. So they confused the Greek 'dead' — *nekros* — with the Latin for 'black' — *niger* — as to their untutored minds the two sounded almost alike. This made them mistranslate necromancy as 'black art'.

Thumbs Up

'Thumbs up' as a symbol of approval and encouragement, too, became such by mistake! To add to the confusion, whoever makes the sign, does so wrongly. In spite of speaking of 'thumb*s* up', he will use only one thumb and not both, as suggested by the plural of the phrase.

Originally, the showing of a thumb — in whichever direction — meant death! It goes back to the Roman gladiatorial fights in which the fate of the loser was decided by the spectators. According to the usual, but incorrect version, it was the practice that if they admired the courage and valour of the defeated man and took pity on him, they turned their thumbs up. This indicated that his life should be spared. However, if their verdict was death, they conveyed the fatal message by their down-turned thumbs, immediately to be followed by the man's execution.

Common sense should suggest the impossibility of such system of signalling. It would be most difficult for those carrying out the sentence to distinguish from afar, in which direction the thumbs pointed.

The mistake arose from a mistranslation of the authentic ancient records. These told that the gesture made in the condemnation of the loser was showing 'a turned thumb' (*pollice verso*). No direction was specified. The phrase was misunderstood and believed to refer to 'a turned *down* thumb'. People then further (wrongly) reasoned that a thumb pointing the other way must signify 'life', and that is how our 'thumbs up' gesture came into existence, the product of mere fiction.

In reality, the gesture used by Roman spectators to save a gladiator's life was to hide their thumbs in their fists. It was known as the 'compressed thumb' (*pollice compresso*). No one could mistake the one for the other. Additionally, both gestures were symbolic. The out-stretched thumb, most probably turned towards the victim, dramatically represented the short Roman sword that almost instantly was going to carry out their sentence. The thumb tucked away, on the other hand, was like a sheathed sword. It was not going to be used.

15 Misquotations —
It Never Said So

Surprising is the number of misquotations commonly used and regarded as authentic. Sometimes the meaning of a text has been essentially distorted by the mere addition or omission of a word or phrase. Other quotations, though absolutely correct, are attributed to the wrong person. There are further examples, in which the wording has been intentionally changed to suit a certain purpose.

'Money is the Root of All Evil'
To say that 'money is the root of all evil' omits an important specification. What St Paul — the author of the observation — actually wrote (in his First Epistle to Timothy, 6:10) was that, 'the love of money is the root of all evil'. Only he who is obsessed by money and worships it makes it a source of unhappiness and evil.

'Charity Begins at Home'
That 'charity begins at home' is a specific type of misquotation. The words are exact and correct. Nothing has been added or left out. But there has been a significant change of meaning in the concept of charity.

As understood now, charity refers to material help. The phrase thus would confirm as man's right, first and foremost to look after 'number one' — himself. The quotation, indeed, has frequently served as a welcome excuse not to contribute or subscribe to outside causes. Such interpretation, however, is far from the original meaning of the phrase. Charity then expressed love in the highest and purest sense. It was the gift of unselfish qualities: compassion, empathy and magnanimity joined with humility. The proper training ground for these traits — once regarded essential for a fulfilling life — was the home, and that was the original implication of 'charity begins at home'.

Power Corrupts

That 'power corrupts' is an unfair generalization and misquotes Lord Acton. What the English historian actually wrote (in a letter to Mandell Creighton dated 5 April 1887) was that 'power tends to corrupt ...' One of the significant qualifications is therefore omitted. His statement claimed that power was conducive to corruption, a dangerous possibility but certainly not — as the misquotation assumes — an inevitable effect.

Battle of Waterloo Won on Playing Fields of Eton

The statement that 'the battle of Waterloo was won on the playing fields of Eton' is generally ascribed to the Duke of Wellington. Knowing the role he had played in the history-making defeat of Napoleon in 1815, his assessment has been quoted as authoritative and well-founded.

Wellington did not say anything of the sort. There is an apocryphal story that, almost ten years after the victory, he had paid a visit to Eton and while watching a cricket match there had been overheard to say, 'The battle of Waterloo was won here.' The exact date of his alleged remark and to whom he addressed it is not mentioned. It is all very vague and it would have been rather odd if Wellington had waited so long to make the acknowledgment.

It is now assumed that the words were first used by the Comte de Montalembert, a French journalist and politician, in a book he published three years after

Wellington's death. In actual fact, only a very few men educated at Eton belonged to Wellington's army.

'A Nation of Shopkeepers'

It is generally assumed that to show his contempt for the English, Napoleon had called them 'a nation of shop-keepers', and this description has been quoted many a time as the emperor's 'original' observation. In reality, he did not coin the phrase which can be traced back to a political treatise by Josiah Tucker which appeared in 1766, three years before Napoleon was born! Whether he ever used it himself is a matter of conjecture.

Napoleon had studied Adam Smith's *Wealth of Nations*, a work in which the Scottish economist discussed whether 'to found a great empire for the sole purpose of raising up a people of customers' was a project fit only for 'a nation of shopkeepers'. It has been suggested that Smith had culled the relevant phrase from Tucker's pamphlet and that — in turn — Napoleon could have quoted Smith, applying the words to the British.

However, the only authentic record of Napoleon ever having thought of the English as a nation of shopkeepers comes from his doctor. He recollects in his *Napoleon in Exile or A Voice from St Helena* a conversation in which the exiled emperor had expressed agreement with a Corsican patriot's opinion to that effect.

'History is Bunk'

That 'history is bunk' is a statement attributed to Henry Ford. He is said to have made it on the witness stand in a libel action against the *Chicago Tribune* at Mt Clemens, Michigan, in July 1919. Questioned in later years whether these were really his words, he could not recollect ever having used them, most definitely not 'bunk'. He nevertheless admitted that, although as far as he could remember the words were not his, they reflected his opinion.

'And Yet, it Does Move'

'And yet, it does move!' are the famous words with which Galileo is said to have defiantly recanted his submission to the Court of the Inquisition. He had uttered them after he had been forced into recognizing as 'true' the teaching of the Church that the earth was the immovable centre of the universe, something he knew to be incorrect.

There are two versions of the incident. One tells that Galileo had only whispered the words to a friend after having put his signature to the ignominious document. The other claims that loudly and daringly he had called out his denial when rising from his knees.

The fact is that no contemporaneous source records the event. The earliest known account of the alleged words appeared 128 years after his repudiation, in *Querelles litteraires,* published by Abbé Trailh in Paris in 1761. It might well be that Galileo's admirers invented the incident to save his scientific integrity.

'Gilding the Lily'

'To gild the lily' has become an accepted 'Shakespearean' phrase, speaking of the unnecessary further adornment of something that is already beautiful. Shakespeare never used the simile in these words. What he spoke of (in *King John,* Act IV, scene 2) was the 'wasteful and ridiculous excess' involved 'to gild refined gold, to paint the lily'. It was like throwing perfume on the violet.

The context is historically significant. King John, who had usurped the throne after his brother's death, realized his ever-growing unpopularity. Anxious to gain the people's esteem and affection, he imagined that a second crowning would do so. But his scheme was rejected by the Earl of Salisbury as utterly futile. He was already king and to have yet another coronation would be like 'painting the lily'.

The Danger of a Little Knowledge

The well-known epigram that 'a little knowledge is a

dangerous thing' misquotes Alexander Pope, its author.
What he actually wrote (in 1711) in his *Essay on Criticism*
was that 'a little learning is a dangerous thing'.

The Better Mousetrap

The observation, 'If a man makes a better mousetrap
than his neighbour, though he builds his house in the
woods, the world will make a beaten path to his door', is
popularly attributed to Ralph Waldo Emerson.
However, none of his works contains the quotation.

It has been suggested that the minister of a New York
church had been the first to use the 'better mousetrap', as
an illustration in one of his sermons. He had done so, not
least, to please a prominent member of his congregation,
a Mr Jay Gould, who had actually invented a new and
'better' mousetrap!

That Emerson was given the credit might have a
possible explanation. For his many lectures, he made use
of thoughts he had jotted down in his *Journals*. These
contain a somewhat lengthy reflection on the
circumstances of fame. This expressed the view that 'If a
man has good corn, or wood, or boards, or pigs to sell, or
can make better chairs or knives, crucibles or church
organs, than anybody else, you will find a broad hard-
beaten road to his house though it be in the woods.' The
words obviously express the same idea as the much more
concise reference to the better mousetrap. The New York
preacher might have paraphrased the passage, adapting it
to his purpose.

'Elementary, My Dear Watson'

Everyone believes that the phrase 'Elementary, my dear
Watson' was a favourite of Sherlock Holmes, used by
him on countless occasions. Whenever crimes baffled
others, he knew the obvious solution which, though overlooked by them, was so 'elementary' to his astute mind.

Actually, the phrase does not appear anywhere in
Conan Doyle's books on Holmes. Only once (in *The*

Crooked Man) does the detective voice the opinion of something as being 'elementary', doing so in reply to Watson's amazement at his power of deduction. Even in this one instance Holmes did not add the now so familiar 'my dear Watson'.

'By the Sweat of his Brow'

'By the sweat of his brow' is a phrase the majority of people wrongly believe to be a literal quotation from the Bible. The relevant passage (Gen. 3:19) however, reads, 'By the sweat of your *face* you shall eat bread'. No one has been able to trace who first misquoted the Bible, as it were lifting (the sweat from) the 'face' to the 'brow'.

'By the Skin of his Teeth'

It was as recent as the last century that a Scottish scientist proved the existence of a skin on man's teeth. Visible only under the microscope, it easily wears off. All the more surprising is the fact that, thousands of years earlier, the book of Job assumed its existence, using it as one of its forceful expressions.

When Job tried to convey to his friends how only the smallest margin had separated him from death, he said to them (Job 19:20), 'I escaped with the skin of my teeth'. Universally now, the passage is rendered as saying, 'I escaped *by* the skin of my teeth'.

The Mess of Pottage

Proverbial is 'the mess of pottage' for which Esau is said to have sold his birthright to his twin-brother Jacob. However, the Bible does not mention any 'mess' of pottage or that Jacob purchased the 'rights' of a first-born at the price of a hurried one-course meal.

The scriptural story (Gen. 25:29-37) differs essentially. When Esau returned from one of his hunts, he felt faint from hunger. Seeing his brother cooking a lentil stew, he asked him for a helping. Jacob cunningly took advantage of the situation. He would let him share the meal, but 'first sell me your birthright'. The Bible does not say that Esau sold him his rights for the price of the food. All it mentions is that, prior to letting Esau eat, Jacob wanted to finalize the transfer of rights.

At the time, Esau could not care less. All he was interested in was to still his hunger — to 'gulp down' some of that 'red stuff'. For, 'of what use is a birthright to me?'

Early readers of the Bible did not misquote it nor misunderstand the text. They actually wondered what Jacob gave Esau to obtain his privileges as the first-born son. Some commentators suggested that 'Jacob paid Esau in cash'. Others claimed that he gave him Methuselah's sword which he had treasured as an heirloom, well realizing that, as a hunter, Esau would value it more than any amount of money.

'Spare the Rod and Spoil the Child'

'Spare the rod and spoil the child' is yet another maxim in which the original (biblical) text is distorted. The actual words (in Proverbs 13:24) say that, 'a father who spares the rod, hates his son', or in the Authorized Version, 'chastens him betimes'.

No doubt Samuel Butler, the English seventeenth-century satiric poet, had this passage in mind when in his poem 'Hudibras' he wrote, 'Spare the rod and spoil the child'. People adopting Butler's paraphrase imagined it was a literal quotation from Scripture, and further misinterpreted it as a biblical injunction to practise unmitigated harshness in the upbringing of a child.

Mohammed and the Mountain

Though of little consequence, it is nevertheless surprising how frequently famous remarks are inaccurately quoted. Recalling an incident in Mohammed's life, Francis Bacon is said to have observed that 'if the mountain will not come to Mohammed, Mohammed must go to the mountain'. The essayist never referred to a resistant mountain. He spoke of an immovable hill.

16 School Howlers, Freudian Slips and Spoonerisms

As mistakes are not confined to any one nation, language or age group, so there are many types of 'lapses'. Slips of the tongue, the wrong choice of word and a peculiar misplacement of letters provide an interesting fund of information and fun. Errors, as well, whether in speech or action (or its neglect) have been shown as revealing 'give-aways' of people's thoughts and character. They lead from the elementary school to the analyst's couch and, indeed, have perpetuated the name of a clergyman who doubled up as a university teacher.

School Howlers

Hilarious are the numerous blunders committed by school children in their work. To relate them has proved such a source of fun that they have become a rewarding part of comedians' repertoires. 'School howlers', as they were termed, are a special category in the world of errors, mistakes innocently made by children with the only effect that they make people laugh heartily. Their number is so great that only a few telling examples must suffice.

• A class of adolescents was told to compose a letter to the local Council requesting more recreational facilities for teenagers. In her draft, one of the girls asked the Council 'to provide more pleasure for teenagers in their pubic (public) areas'.

• After attending a service at church, children were requested to relate their experience in an essay. Rather critically, one pupil recorded that he had had great difficulty in hearing the preacher, as the agnostics (acoustics) in the church were terrible.

● A little boy asked by his mate why he did not come to his church, explained that he belonged to another 'abomination' (denomination).

● In an essay on Johann Sebastian Bach, a schoolboy described him as 'a most prolific composer' who was the father of twenty children and who, in his spare time, 'practised in the attic on a spinster (spinet)'.

● Asked by the history teacher to illustrate the popularity of the Duke of Wellington, a pupil referred to his 'glorious funeral' — 'it took six men to carry the beer (bier)'.

● A student discussing the value of primitive art in modern studies, epitomized his view by stating that 'studies of art have contributed mush (much) to anthropology'.

Other 'howlers' spoke of tundras as 'treeless forests in South America' and called Genesis, the first book of the Bible, 'Guinesses'. Sins of omission were explained as those 'we have forgotten to commit'.

● One pupil, proud of his community's low rate of traffic fatalities, which he hoped would be emulated at other places, recalled that 'it has been about a year since the town had a fertility'.

● A famous general was described as 'a battle-scared (scarred) warrior'! In correcting the mistake, the valiant soldier was changed into a 'bottle-scarred' hero.

● Dealing with ancient history, a child related how the 'Carthaginians won (!) their first defeat'.

● Zoology has had its share of blunders. Rabies was defined as 'Jewish priests' (rabbis) and marsupials described as 'poached animals'.

● Memorable, too, are specifically Australian school howlers. They include statements like 'the people squatted and then grew wheat'; 'there was soil erosion on the river bank until the government stepped in'; 'the cow usually produces more milk than its father did' and 'the people who started plantations were Europeans from America'.

● Was it a future doctor or an aspiring author who defined an appendix as a portion of a book which nobody has yet discovered to be of any use? Yet another pupil referred to the liver as an 'infernal organ'.

● Asked to write in clearer English badly worded statements, a ten-year-old girl 'improved' the sentence, 'If the baby does not thrive on fresh milk, it should be boiled' to read, 'If the baby does not thrive on fresh milk, it should be killed'. Maybe she had watched too many horrendous TV movies.

● Paradise was explained as 'what happens to you when your arms go stiff'. King Solomon, certainly, would have been a much happier man if a student's account had been correct that the Old Testament monarch 'apart from his many wives kept 700 porcupines (concubines)'.

● Defining the difference between a king and a president, a pupil wrote that whilst the king was the son of his father, 'the president isn't'.

At times, parents do not lag far behind their children in contributing to the store of howlers. An Italian migrant child had missed classes because of an attack of migraine. In a letter of apology, her mother explained that she was sorry Dominica has been absent from school, but 'she has been having migrants, which are very painful'.

Freudian Slips
Modern psychology has shown an important aspect of many mistakes which so far had been overlooked. Errors are not always as innocent and insignificant as at first they appear. They may well be the unconscious confession of concealed feelings, suppressed desires and hidden intentions. The mistake that gives them away can take a diversity of forms and be in the nature of a forgotten date, a mispronounced word or a simple misspelling. As it were, one single letter omitted, might speak volumes.

Professor Sigmund Freud in his *Psychopathology of Everyday Life* was among the very first to point to the revealing nature of errors. Not a mere accident caused a slip of the tongue or the lapse of mind. They had some underlying reason.

Examples abound and occur in almost every sphere of life. There was the young student of theology who, taking a service, loudly and distinctly praised God as 'the source of immorality'.

• In a discussion on the meaning of adolescence, a youth who, at the time, himself was passing through that very phase, defined it as 'the stage between puberty and adultery'.

• A lady secretary typing the draft of a new magazine to be called The *Progressive Mail,* misspelled its title to read The *Progressive Male.*

• A signwriter, commissioned to paint a warning post to trespassers, 'slipped'. The board threatened that 'Violators will be prostituted'.

• A story is told of Lord Curzon who, when Secretary of State for Foreign Affairs in the British Cabinet, had received a communication from Greece complaining that the monks at Mount Athos were violating their vows. In the transcript, the vows had been misspelled as cows. With his tongue in cheek, Curzon is said to have annotated the message by instructing his office to 'send them a Papal bull'.

• Acknowledging the generous donation by a member of the municipality, the secretary of the Council informed the donor that it was proposed to use the money to purchase 'new wenches (benches) for our park, as the present old ones are in a very dilapidated state'.

Freud himself has provided an abundance of examples illustrating the phenomenon. At his own expense, he recalled an incident in his practice. After the consultation, a patient asked for the amount of the fee (which, in fact, he had already ascertained from the analyst's secretary). He did not like to owe any money, he said, especially not to a doctor, adding, 'I prefer to play right away'. According to Freud's theory, the underlying motive of his slip of the tongue — changing the 'pay' into 'play' — was only too obvious. Nevertheless and contrary to expectation, the patient took out his wallet to 'pay' the stipulated sum. After having put down £2 however, he stopped, explaining that he must have left the rest of the money at home. He promised to mail it the moment he had returned to his office. There is no need to complete the story. The money never arrived. The case well supported a psychiatrist's observation that it was not accidental that we are more apt to mislay letters containing accounts than cheques.

Freud quotes the self-revealing remark of a domineering wife whose husband was recovering from sickness. She told her friends that he had not to follow any specific diet and could eat 'what *I* want'.

To the same type of Freudian slips belonged a henpecked husband's request to his wife. On a Sunday morning at the breakfast table she had accused him of shirking his duties. Instead of helping her in washing the dishes and tidying up the house after the previous night's party, all he thought about was his game of golf! Assuring her that nothing was farther from his mind, he asked her with almost the same breath, 'Please, pass me the putter'.

Mistakes thus can reveal our unconscious thoughts. That forgotten appointment, the overlooked birthday, the anniversary we just did not remember 'because I was so busy' might, after all, be a confession of lost interest and waned affection.

Spoonerisms

A curious form of mistakes is the accidental transposition of letters, syllables or words, putting them where they do not belong. A 'butterfly' thus is turned into a 'flutterby' and a 'crushing blow' becomes a 'blushing crow'.

Somehow lines get crossed and normal channels of communication between the mind and the tongue break down. Commands sent from the speech centre in the brain are either delayed or arrive too early and, by lack of synchronization, with the tongue unable to cope, speech gets twisted. Scientifically, the phenomenon is termed 'metathesis'. A Greek word, it simply expresses the 'change of position'. But because the Reverend William A. Spooner (1844–1930), a well-known English clergyman and for many years Warden of New College, Oxford, was particularly prone to making such mistakes, they have been called by his name — Spoonerisms.

Numerous are the examples attributed to him, though each needs careful examination as to its authenticity. The comic effect was too inviting not to tempt people to manufacture spurious 'quotations', i.e. Spoonerisms which were not Spooner's at all but invented.

Some of the most popular were addressed to his students. 'You deliberately tasted two worms', Spooner reprimanded one of his charges. What, of course, he meant to say was that the student had deliberately 'wasted two terms'. 'You can leave Oxford by the down train', was twisted to 'by the town drain'. 'You hissed my mystery lecture', was yet another of his blunders.

Spooner made a number of other mistakes in his ecclesiastical capacity. When at the end of the wedding ceremony a nervous bridegroom forgot to fulfil one of the traditional customs, the helpful Dr Spooner reminded him that it was 'kisstomary to cuss the bride'. Well-known is his announcement of the hymn 'When conquering Kings their titles take', as 'When kinkering Kongs their titles take'. God, the 'loving shepherd' became the 'shoving leopard'. Spooner stopped a female congregant from entering a reserved pew by politely informing her, 'Mardon me, Padam, this pie is occupewed.' Offering his assistance, he added, 'Allow me to scw you to another sheet.'

Further transpositions on Spooner's part concerned his view on life, historical figures and moments. 'We all know,' Spooner observed, 'what it is to have a half-warmed fish within us', indeed a memorable reversal of a half-formed wish. Queen Victoria became 'our queer old dean'. To give soldiers returning from war service in France a proper welcome, he suggested, 'When the boys come back, we'll have the hags flung out.' The 'sons of toil' changed into 'tons of soil' and 'smelling salts' became 'selling smalts'.

Spooner's peculiarity in speech must have had a reason. It has been suggested that a combination of circumstances might have been responsible. He was an albino who also suffered from weak eyesight, conditions that made him nervous and could have resulted in his speech affliction. However, there are other explanations.

To begin with, Spooner may have made such an amusing and 'memorable' slip of the tongue quite accidentally. Realizing its effect on his listeners, he came to produce such misplacements of words intentionally, as a sort of gimmick. Probably, he also enjoyed the mental effort it took, so much so that his habit developed into an addiction.

Being only human, it is not unlikely that Spooner loved to show off his mental agility, the lightning speed of his thoughts, able to transform a common expression into something 'different'. Thus it may have become an affectation. Certainly, ordinary words of a preacher or teacher are quickly forgotten, but not so a mistake, particularly if it was so clever and sounded so funny.

17 Deadly Mistakes

No period of life has been without its mistakes. It is no wonder then that dying and death which, after all, are an integral part of everyone's life, have not been exempted. Fatal mistakes, as it were, live on in our culture and heritage. When the German painter Liebermann discussed his work with the equally famous surgeon Sauerbruch, he is said to have remarked, 'You bury your mistakes, but mine are hung on the wall for all to see.'

An inquest into errors concerned with death, in the many forms they have taken, indeed offers intriguing evidence of the oddest kind of survival.

Dead Reckoning

Death — so ubiquitous — has even intruded spheres where it does not belong. Its presence in naval terminology is merely fictitious. There is nothing fatal in 'dead reckoning'.

A system of measuring at sea, its deadly association has been totally misunderstood. For many centuries, when still lacking modern navigational aids, boats far away from land charted their course by purely theoretical calculations. They established their position by taking into account the distance and direction they had travelled, making due allowance for currents and tidal streams. For at least 400 years, this system was described as '*ded*uced reckoning'. As this was a rather lengthy and learned term, sailors shortened it. Both in speech and in their logbook entry, they referred to it as 'ded. reckoning', a description which to ordinary people made no sense. Not realizing that *ded* was an abbreviation, they wrongly took it to stand for 'dead'.

Others believe that 'dead' reckoning went back much further, to the very days when large parts of the ocean were still uncharted Not knowing how far the waters reached, sailors then referred to the 'unknown sea' as 'dead'.

Threats of Suicide

That those who threaten to commit suicide never do so, is a fallacy and a dangerous generalization. Certainly, some people use such threat as psychological blackmail to achieve an objective, if only to attract attention or to be pitied. They never intend taking their lives. However, in many cases those who speak of putting an end to their lives, really mean it and their talk might well be a call of distress which should not be ignored. Records have shown that in the majority of suicides or suicide attempts the individual had previously made known his or her intention.

Life Flashing Past at Death

A wide-spread popular notion claims that at the moment of death, particularly so from drowning, a man's entire life flashed past him. It is an assertion which, obviously, is difficult to prove or deny. Nevertheless, people who could have been described as actually dying, but escaped death by the narrowest margin — being resuscitated or rescued — have testified that they did not experience the phenomenon. Instead, they had focused their mind, in what they assumed to be their last moments, on a desperate attempt to save themselves.

Hair and Nails Growing After Death

Macabre and mistaken is the belief that the hair of a dead person keeps on growing. At death all enzymes are destroyed and, with it, all growth ceases.

The wrong impression is due to faulty observation.

After death, the flesh shrinks and the skin, by contracting towards the hair roots, makes the hair stand out more conspicuously. This creates the illusion that it has grown. Equally fanciful is a similar assumption concerning a deceased person's nails. They do not grow after death either.

Spreading Plague by Prayer

Facing desperate situations, men have committed fatal mistakes. Instead of halting disaster, they intensified it. This applied particularly to the plague. Ravaging entire communities, it led to the deaths of thousands. Men saw in the scourge divine punishment for their sins. Crowding the churches to ask for God's forgiveness and help, they spread the infection all the more!

Error of judgment was not confined to the common people but extended to London's Lord Mayor — with equally disastrous consequences. Blaming the many dogs and cats roaming the streets of the city for the epidemic, he embarked on a campaign to have them all destroyed. He did not realize that the animals exterminated had killed the rats that had carried the fleas which spread the infection! Instead of stopping the plague, his measures caused an enormous increase in the number of victims, further decimating the population of London.

The Toadstool

However much its name might suggest, the toadstool has no link with the warty creature. Derived from the German, its description refers to 'death' (*Tod*) which has its 'seat' (*Stuhl*) in the poisonous fungus.

A Life Sentence

Man has always tried to embellish the unpleasant, not least by the use of euphemisms. A 'life insurance' thus provides for the death of a person. On the other hand, a 'life sentence' once meant what it said. The condemned criminal was to be imprisoned to the very last day of his life — until death. Though man's life expectancy has considerably increased, the duration of a life sentence has been reduced. It now rarely exceeds twenty years, making its description redundant and incorrect.

Judge's Black Cap

When the death penalty was still part of the criminal code, the judge passing the sentence, used ceremoniously to cover his head with what came to be known as a 'black cap'. In reality, this was not a cap but a square of black silk meant to symbolize his sorrow in having to condemn the criminal to die. Early custom decreed that the judge had to don the cap once again, when his sentence was about to be 'executed'.

Shibboleth

Shibboleth is a most fateful word. Though used today merely for a principle or characteristic which distinguishes a particular class of people or members of a party from another, once it determined whether a man was going to live or die.

It was first applied in biblical times on a specific historical occasion on the shores of the River Jordan. When the Ephraimite army had been routed by the Gileadite forces, their remnant ran for their lives. Knowing that safety beckoned on the other side of the river, they tried to cross it. However, Jephthah, the Gileadites' leader, had anticipated their move and stationed guards on all the fords of the Jordan.

As in those early days uniforms were still unknown, it was difficult to differentiate between friend and foe, making it all the harder to identify the fugitives. A linguistic peculiarity on the part of the defeated forces came to the aid of the victors. The Ephraimites spoke with a distinct accent. As many people nowadays cannot produce the guttural sound of the Scottish lo*ch* and the Chinese change the 'r' into an 'l', so they were unable to voice the 'sh'. Well aware of the Ephraimites' speech impediment, the sentries stopped everyone wanting to cross the Jordan. If he asserted to be a Gileadite, to verify his claim, they asked him to repeat after them *shibboleth,* the Hebrew for an 'ear of corn'. If he was a fugitive, he pronounced the word *sibboleth*. His tongue gave him away and he was killed on the spot.

The Swan Song

Poetically, the last performance of a great artist is known as (his or her) swan song. The romantic figure of speech goes back to ancient legend, according to which a dying swan burst forth in glorious song.

Greek myth featured the swan as Apollo's bird. It is no wonder therefore that the god had endowed it with a magnificent voice. It was equally not surprising that the bird, joyfully, used it at its very best at the moment of death, when about to join its master who, after all, had so blessed it.

Swans, of course, never sing. Although, almost 2,000 years ago, in his *Natural History* the Roman writer Pliny had pointed out the fallacy, his words went unheeded. Poets and dramatists, once again among them Shakespeare, continued to give credence to the myth and to perpetuate it in their works. Because of their authority, its authenticity was not doubted.

There might be a rational explanation of the fanciful swan song. People were mystified by the weird, prolonged death rattle the dying bird produced, when its expiring breath slowly passed through its elongated windpipe. Man has always given much thought to death and dying. Piously, if not wishfully, he felt that it need not be destructive or tragic, in fact nothing to be feared. He therefore beautified those last moments of passing away — whether from the public eye or from the stage of life. He imagined to hear a jubilant note in the generally terrifying sound of death, thus creating the swan song. It made Byron express the wish of most men, 'Swanlike, let me sing and die.'